together

Also by Judy Goldman

NONFICTION
Losing My Sister

FICTION
Early Leaving
The Slow Way Back

POETRY
Wanting to Know the End
Holding Back Winter

together

a memoir of a marriage
and a medical mishap

Judy Goldman

NAN A. TALESE

Doubleday
New York

Portions of this work originally appeared in the following
publications: "Holding Back Winter" in *Holding Back Winter*
(St. Andrews Press, 1987); "Love in North Carolina" in
Best Creative Nonfiction of the South (Texas Review Press, 2017);
and "Finger on the Trigger" in *drafthorse* (Winter 2016).

Book design by Maria Carella
Jacket design by Michael J. Windsor
Jacket photograph courtesy of the author

Library of Congress Cataloging-in-Publication Data
Names: Goldman, Judy (Poet) author.
Title: Together : a memoir of a marraige and a medical mishap /
by Judy Goldman
Description: First edition. | New York : Nan A. Talese /
Doubleday, 2019.
Identifiers: LCCN 2017060152 | ISBN 9780385543941
(hardcover) | ISBN 9780385543958 (ebook)
Subjects: LCSH: Goldman, Judy (Poet)—Marriage. | Authors,
American—20th century—Biography. | Woman authors—20th
century—Biography. | Medical errors—United States.
Classification: LCC PS3557.O3688 Z46 2019 | DDC 811/.54 [B]—dc23
LC record available at https://lccn.loc.gov/2017060152

MANUFACTURED IN THE UNITED STATES OF AMERICA

1 3 5 7 9 10 8 6 4 2

First Edition

For Henry

Once and for all, let me say it here:
I am the lucky one.

For one human being to love another human being: that is perhaps the most difficult task that has been entrusted to us, the ultimate task, the final test and proof, the work for which all other work is merely preparation. That is why young people, who are beginners in everything, are not yet capable of love: it is something they must learn. With their whole being, with all their forces gathered around their solitary, anxious, upward-beating hearts, they must learn to love.

—*Rainer Maria Rilke, in a letter to the nineteen-year-old Franz Xaver Kappus*

The secret of a happy marriage remains a secret.

—*Henny Youngman*

together

1

Henry and I are at the kitchen table, eating breakfast. Grape-Nuts, sliced banana, milk for him. Oatmeal for me, with walnuts chopped small, fresh blueberries, and dried cranberries. Mugs of coffee. I did not always drink coffee. My feeling was that it never tasted as good as it smelled. But with enough half and half, I like it now. Funny about how we describe ourselves. One minute, we're: *Oh, I'm not a coffee drinker. Never touch it.* The next, we're solidly in another camp: *Have to have coffee every morning.* Who we are can flip like that. The details always shifting. Henry picks up the Sports section, folds it in half, then half again, pushes the rest of *The Charlotte Observer* to the far side of the table. I've got the Living section. It's mid-February 2006. Outside: wintry and windy. And wet.

"Doesn't this sound like a good idea?" he says, pointing to an ad I can't read from where I'm sitting. "A nonsurgical procedure for back pain. Done by a physiatrist."

"What's a physiatrist?" I ask, scooting my chair closer so that I can read even the fine print.

"According to the ad, physiatrists are MDs," he says. "Apparently, they treat spinal problems."

Six years ago, Henry had surgery for spinal stenosis, which helped some. But his back has never really stopped hurting. He's stiff when he gets out of bed in the morning. Can't stand for long, finds a chair pretty quickly wherever he happens to be. He lives a normal life, though. A normal life with backaches. He's so athletic, what he'd really like is to be able to jog again, play racquetball, tennis.

Yes, I say, that *does* sound like a good idea.

.

The physiatrist tells Henry he believes he can help. From what I can understand, he'll use fluoroscopy for guidance while he injects steroids and an anesthetic into the epidural space—between the spine and the spinal cord. The procedure will take about thirty minutes, followed by maybe forty-five minutes of recovery time. Henry will be monitored for an additional fifteen to twenty minutes, then discharged to go home. An hour and a half—total! Compare this to hours on an operating table, days in the hospital, the long recuperation that back surgery entails. This injection is so common, it's given to women during childbirth. The physiatrist explains that an epidural steroid injection can be highly effective because it delivers pain relief directly to the source of the problem. He recommends two injections, spaced three weeks apart; he needs to inject two different areas. As with all invasive procedures, there are risks. Generally, though, the risks are few and tend to be rare: headache, infection, bleeding, nerve damage.

Henry signs the consent form.

·

A week later, we report to the hospital outpatient clinic for the first epidural. Afterward, Henry's right leg is numb. Very little feeling. The physiatrist, a tall fellow with a friendly face and thick, hay-colored hair anyone would envy, says something like "The numbness is a great sign! It means the epidural is working!"

Henry's leg is so numb he can barely walk. He leans on me as I help him from the car into our house and to our bed. He goes right to sleep, which is unusual for him. I don't think I've ever seen him take a nap. The little bit of walking he did completely exhausted him. I keep checking the handout: *If numbness persists longer than eight hours, call the office.* Every hour, I wake Henry to ask about the numbness. Every hour, he says his leg is still numb. Then he drifts back off. I don't relax my shoulders for a minute. The eighth hour, I have my hand on the phone, ready to dial. I ask him one last time. All feeling has returned. No need to call. My shoulders relax.

His second epidural is scheduled for three weeks from now.

·

But first our vacation, planned months ago, on the French side of the island of St. Martin. The romance of spending long days in two chaises pulled close, our bare toes touching, how warm we are from the sun, lost in our books. Less than a hundred feet away, our lunch place juts out over the sea, the smoky grill, the smell of fresh-caught fish cooking.

Evenings, we stroll the rutted mile from our small resort to the row of Caribbean-colored, gingerbread-cottage restaurants. Henry's back is still hurting, so we have to stop every now and then for him to stretch—backward, forward, bending way over, hands on knees—but a little pain is not going to keep him from what he wants to do. The moon's soft light catches the sea grape leaves all around us. We debate the menus posted on the little front porches. Our main concern: Are we in the mood for mussels or sole?

·

Seven days after St. Martin, we leave early for our one-forty-five appointment at the same hospital out-patient clinic as before. It's one of those golden North Carolina days that always make me wonder why any-one would ever want to live anywhere else. Pure sun-light, air fragrant.

Henry checks in. There are so many people here, the waiting room feels tight. The only available chairs together are catty-corner, a square table in between. But no sooner do we sit down than a nurse comes to take Henry back. She has an air of efficiency about her—the way she holds her head and her shoulders, her sensible nurse shoes. I didn't know anybody still wore those. She says she'll call for me in a few minutes, after they get him ready; I can keep him company while he waits for the doctor. I pick up *People* magazine and settle in, even though I don't recognize the names of any of the celebrities.

I glance at my watch. How did it get to be three o'clock? Why aren't they coming for me?

At three-thirty, a nurse—not the same one who took him back, but a shiny-faced young woman, perky, smiley—appears and says that my husband has had the epidural.

"Oh," I say, "I thought somebody was going to come get me so I could be with him before—"

"Well," she says, "we're real busy today, and things got sorta hectic back there, and then the doctor was all of a sudden ready for him around three o'clock, and we never had a chance to come get you."

I walk behind her down the long hall. She's repeating, brightly, "Your husband's verrry numb! Verrry numb!" as though she's marveling over some unusual turn of events, more amusing, really, than anything to worry about.

"He's numb?" I ask, trying to match her brightness, wondering why my little laugh is coming out shaky.

She stops outside a closed door. Pauses. Opens it. I follow her in.

When she moves to the side and Henry is in full view, I see that he's flat on his back on a gurney, a sheet pulled up around his neck, the way you'd tuck in a child. His expression is contorted. His whole face an agonized flinch. As though he took the world head-on and lost.

"Judy," he whispers, his eyes clutching at mine, "I can't feel a thing from my waist down. I can't move my legs."

I turn to the nurse. "Where's the doctor?" My voice rises with each word, going someplace totally unfamiliar. "Does the doctor know?"

"Well," she says, "not exactly."

"He needs to see this!" My voice verges on shrill. My hand brushes the air. "Go. Get the doctor. Please! Ask him to come in here!"

She's backing out of the room.

I'm shivering.

.

I sit down beside Henry, put my hand on his arm. I don't know where to touch him, if it's even okay to touch him.

"Tell me," I say.

He says that when the doctor was giving the injection, he felt severe pain. He must have groaned, because the doctor asked him, Are you okay? He told the doctor, No, I'm not okay. I'm in excruciating pain. The doctor said, We're almost done. Then he finished the injection.

Henry tells me that his back, where the needle went in, still hurts.

Maybe it's not as bad as I'm terrified that it is. Maybe he's really all right. Maybe I can *help* him be all right. Maybe what's been taken away can be brought back. I just have to figure this out. But I need to hurry. Before it—whatever *it* is—locks into place.

I loosen the sheet around his feet.

"Can you feel this?" I scratch his bare toes.

"No," he says. "Not at all." He sounds as though he's grown tired somewhere deep in his body.

"Can you wiggle your toes?"

"I'm trying. Are they moving?"

They aren't. I wiggle them myself, to get them started. But then, nothing.

"Can you flex this foot? Or this one?"

"I can't make either one move."

"How about your leg?" I tap his knee through the sheet. "Can you lift your leg? Can you lift it just a little? This one? Or this one?"

"I'm trying, I'm trying as hard as I can."

I stroke the tops of his feet, then the soles, with my fingers. For a second, I think how another time, another place, I might run my hand down his calf to his foot. Maybe in the morning, on my way to the bathroom, rounding the bed, I might reach under the sheet and touch the bottom of his foot. That careless, offhanded thing married people do.

"What about this?" I ask, massaging his ankles. "Can you feel me doing this?"

"I can't."

Now I'm reaching under the sheet and rubbing his calves.

No.

I reach farther and touch his knees, thighs, groin, buttocks.

No, no, no, no.

He feels nothing.

I feel everything.

.

One minute you're complaining that the zinc-based sunscreen you're supposed to wear in the Caribbean goes on like Elmer's Glue. The next, you're Googling *paralysis*. Everything is okay. Then nothing is. That thin line. How a brushfire can erupt on a perfectly sunny, clear-skied day. How your life can be taken right out of your hands.

2

Barrel-chested, bruiser Henry—I always loved that he
was so big and strong and brave. Sensitive and kind-
hearted, yes (my friends say he's the most "evolved"
of all our husbands, the one most likely to join a cluster of women talking, the one most likely to get up at
night with a fussy baby), but if you met him, your first
impression would be sturdiness. Sturdy is what I must
have been after when I married him. Not consciously,
of course. But it was probably on my checklist.

As a child, I was slight, *not* athletic, *not* known
for physical strength, *not* brave. My grandpa called
me Flimely, a Yiddish word meaning *little bird*. That
image of me stuck. I was sweet. Demure. Too small
to be taken seriously. Or, at least, that's how I saw
myself. Everyone else saw me that way, too. My sister,
Brenda, three years older, was the strong one. It's how
she defined herself. The rest of us believed deeply in
that definition, too. I can't remember a time when she
wasn't big. (Was she *born* five-eight?)

My mother rewarded me for being me with all the
attention in the world. Maybe because I'd nearly died

when I was born. Maybe because I was the baby of the family, youngest of three, an accident she forever after expressed gratitude for. ("What would we do without our Judy?")

We continued to see me as a little bird, even as I was growing up, cutting away, becoming independent, actually showing strength. Then, like many women of my generation, I married and made myself at home in the role of Looked-After Wife. I had a husband. I felt safe. I think I probably saw myself as lucky to snag a man so brawny.

In any marriage, one person becomes the _____ one (fill in the blank), and the other person becomes something in tandem. (Similar to my sister and me.) Henry would be the protector. I'd be the protected. Husbands and wives (like siblings) assume they do not possess the central quality the other possesses. If Henry is strong, I must not be. He can shield me forever. I did the same thing Patty Hearst did— married my bodyguard. Or maybe I married a person who would join me in re-creating the family I grew up in.

3

A knock on the door. The physiatrist bursts in.

"I gave you the Saddam shot!" he says to Henry, with great enthusiasm. His face, his gesturing, everything about him is as spirited as the nurse who brought me into this room.

"What's a Saddam shot?" I ask, hoping his answer will explain everything—the look on Henry's face, the feeling that there's a cold hand on the back of my neck.

"I gave him the mother of all shots! Very potent!" he says. His smile is wide, natural. Another time, another place, I might say he's charming. "In fact, I gave him two shots!" Later I'll see there are two small Band-Aids on Henry's back, covering two injection sites.

"But he can't move his legs." That's me, trying to ask a million questions but not knowing how to ask even one. "What if he doesn't—?"

"Your husband is going to be all right," he says. "It'll just be a matter of time."

"He'll be okay?"

"He'll be fine."

I glance over at Henry. He's not saying a word. His expression is flat and abstracted. As if there's nothing in the conversation he can grab hold of. This husband of mine, who's usually so attentive, so engaged in talk, who could go on and on for hours with our daughter about the quickest way to drive from our house to Costco without hitting a light, who could talk for hours with anyone about anything that interests him (and most things do interest him)—where is he now?

"Don't you worry," the doctor is saying. "We've seen this before."

A little more back and forth between the two of us. And he leaves the room. It's four o'clock. Two and a half hours since we arrived for the appointment.

Our same nurse—the perky one—breezes back in, carrying paper-wrapped tubes and instruments in the fold of her arms. She catheterizes Henry, gives him a shot of Demerol to "take the edge off," leaves again, then almost immediately rushes back in.

"Oh, the doctor ordered an MRI," she says to Henry, "but the MRI machine is in use, and anyway"—she turns to me—"you're going to have to fill out a bunch of forms before we can even call a transporter, so it'll be a while before your husband can have the scan."

"A transporter?"

"Somebody who'll take him down to Imaging."

"Is there any way to hurry the process along?" I ask. "Does the scheduler in the MRI Department know this is an emergency?"

I'm now placing all my trust in the MRI. Yes, an

MRI will give us the information we need to make everything go back to normal. An MRI will be an action. *Any* action will be an improvement over what we've been doing, just letting time pass. I'm back to my composed, agreeable self, keeping my voice steady—because I want that MRI and I want it now. My mother always said: *Cast your bread upon the waters.* I took that to mean if I'm sweet and polite, the smooth surface of my entitlement will never be shattered. I'll get what I want. Which may not be exactly what the Book of Ecclesiastes was aiming for. Years later, I'll understand that Mother's philosophy is one explanation for why there are these two versions of me: The Judy most familiar to people who know me— the timid, mild-mannered, rule-following, southern Judy who relies on others to get results. And the not-so-well-known Judy, whose strong sense of rightness compels her to take control.

"Why don't you call for a transporter while I'm filling out the forms?" the second Judy asks. "To make things go faster."

"That's a great idea!" the nurse says, as though I've just suggested something that could be a lot of fun. A movie followed by doughnuts. An elevator to the top of the Empire State Building. New shoes. "Let me see what I can do. Maybe I can get the doctor to write *stat* on the request, which would give it emergency status."

The doctor didn't indicate this was an emergency? My husband paralyzed from the waist down is not an emergency?

4

I've always been in love with the mythology surrounding married couples and how they met. I come by this honestly. Everyone in the family I grew up in adored these stories, told them over and over. We always acted as though we were hearing the details for the first time. *And then what happened?* one of us would say. *You're kidding!*

With my parents, it was the opposite of love at first sight. Columbia, South Carolina, 1930, a cotillion with a live band, lights low—my mother, Margaret Bogen, was twenty years old and Cotillion Sweetheart. When the dance was half over, my father, Ben Kurtz, twenty-one, arrived with a carful of buddies. Mother—wearing her beauty like sequins, that short bob, dazzling smile—was slow-dancing with her date. My father cut in, one strong finger jabbing. The story goes that he was drunk, which would have been unusual for him; I never saw him take a drink. But I can picture the way his jaw must have been set, his lean, handsome face, his fervor when he said to her, the instant they started gliding across the floor, "You're just the type I hate. Everybody's sweetheart. Miss Queen of the Ball." Her answer: "*You're* just the type *I* hate. Late to the party. Drunk. Bottle under the table." Months later, a mutual friend introduced them, not knowing about that first encounter. They fell instantly in love.

My sister met her husband (both college freshmen) on a blind date in Atlanta, New Year's Eve. Not exactly the night you want a blind date. But New Year's Day, she called home, breathless. My parents and I listened in on three different extensions—my father in the den, Mother at the phone table in the back hall, me upstairs on the cedar chest on the landing. "He's real good-looking! And tall. And nice!" Oh, the dips and rises of Brenda's voice. I wrote everything down, because I knew we were looking into the future.

Henry and I met on a blind date, too. Only we accelerated the process by becoming engaged on our third date. We literally saw each other three times and decided to get married. We weren't even living in the same town. It was 1967. I was in New York City; he had just moved to Charlotte. Long-distance calls were too expensive, so we wrote letters. What makes our quick engagement, and then our quick marriage, truly bizarre is that neither of us is impulsive. Our friends would probably say we're the most deliberate people they know. We don't change brands of toothpaste without weighing the pros and cons.

How did we get from point A (blind date, April 1967) to point B (engagement, June 1967) to point C (wedding, August 1967)?

We have to go back to June 1963, when my future seemed as sparkly as the diamond on my finger. I had just graduated from the University of Georgia, and in three weeks I would marry Rick, a law student at the University of North Carolina. It would be a grand wedding. I had my eight bridesmaids and the eight beaded evening bags I'd give them at the bridesmaids' luncheon. After our honeymoon, we'd live in a cute little duplex in Chapel Hill; there'd be Saturday-evening cookouts with neighbors; I'd teach at a nearby high school until I got pregnant. Invitations had been mailed. RSVPs checked off. A lacy white wedding gown and veil hung in my closet. Gifts were arriving (ice buckets, silver butter knives, place mats). Only three weeks to go.

That's when I broke the engagement.

I don't believe I was ever in love with Rick, but here's what I liked: his intelligence and kindness, first of all. And he had such devoted friends. (If *they* loved him, shouldn't *I*?) His parents were amiable, homey. My parents must have also thought they were amiable and homey—the four of them had already taken a trip together. As though we were *all* getting married. Since I'd grown up in Rock Hill, South Carolina, where everyone was either Methodist or Baptist, he was really the first Jewish boy I'd dated. I wondered if maybe love was different when it was between two

Jewish people, not so fierce, more a settled-down kind of feeling. And there was that timing: college graduation followed by wedding followed by the rest of my life. Perfect. Well, good enough.

It's how we made decisions in those days. Maybe people still make important decisions based on factors no more solid than a coin toss. *Oh, okay. I'll just get married.*

The end came when Rick and I drove to High Point to buy furniture. That day—despite all the signposts I had watched slip by, including the ring he'd given me on my birthday in October eight months before, despite my engagement picture in the newspaper, planning the wedding and honeymoon, renting the duplex—at that point, on that day, I knew it was time to break the engagement. I'd already let too much time go by; it was now or never.

Here's how I did it: I said no to every piece of furniture in the showroom. Dinette set? No. Tufted sofa? No. Bed? No. Furnitureless, we returned to his parents' house in Charlotte and were alone in the living room. My plan was to deliver the news on his turf, which seemed the only decent thing to do. Let him be as comfortable as possible. The two of us sat side by side on the beige sofa in the house he'd grown up in. I told him I'd made a mistake, I had doubts, I couldn't go through with the wedding. He said maybe it was just cold feet, the planning, the stress, I'd feel more relaxed when the wedding got here. No, I said, you deserve someone who's really in love with you.

"So, this is it?" he finally said, miserably. "This is it," I said, miserably. I felt solid about my decision. But conscience-stricken.

He and his parents drove me back to my parents' house in Rock Hill, his mother and father in the front seat, Rick and me in the back. None of us said a word the entire forty-five-minute drive, as though the shadows in the car separated each of us from the other. I stared hard out my window, into the distance. My head was churning.

When I walked into the house, my parents were sitting on the leather sofa in the den, watching television. They had not expected me till the next day. Still, they beamed, delighted to see me, as though my arrival was just a lovely surprise.

"I broke my engagement," I said, the words pushing out in accelerated breaths, my voice sounding not at all like me, tears filling my eyes. Saying those words out loud, admitting to my parents—to anyone—the secret I'd held tight for eight months felt intensely disloyal to Rick. And shameful. And embarrassing, because of what this said about me and my inability to manage my life. At the same time, admitting my secret felt like balm. My father immediately stood up, walked across the room, that long stride of his. He clicked off the TV, motioned me to sit down next to Mother. He was then on the other side of me. The two of them circled me firmly in their arms.

Mother had long suspected things were not as they seemed. Days after Rick gave me the ring, she looked me in the eye and asked, "Are you sure you're in love?" We were standing in our autumny front yard, next to the concrete bench, solid and fixed under the low branches of the oak tree. There was a chill in the air, even with that bright sun. I can still picture the way she was taking me in. So intent. I wondered if she could read my mind, or my heart. "I'm sure," I said. The only time I ever lied to her.

Now I was telling everything—the seemingly endless months of doubt, the trip to buy furniture, my acquiescing to the inevitable.

Mother's main message: I was brave to do what I did.

I felt the opposite of brave. Why had I let the engagement go on so long? Why had I gotten engaged in the first place? What was wrong with me?

I spent that long summer in Rock Hill, with its thick, humid air, feeling depressed and guilty, set upon by remorse over hurting such a good person. Alone in my room, windows open to the heat, I played an Andy Williams record over and over on my stereo. The first eleven words of the song, my new anthem: "What kind of fool am I, who never fell in love?" I'd had boyfriends in junior high and high school, had loved as deeply as a teenager could love. But now that I was an adult, had I grown incapable of falling in love? The song called into question everything I thought I was.

·

Summer smoothed out into fall, and I applied for a job teaching high school English in Atlanta. I was so late applying, I was afraid there wouldn't be any openings. But Roosevelt High School, the largest high school for white kids in Atlanta, located in one of the poorest neighborhoods, had just been court-ordered to admit black students—one or two per grade, carefully selected and instructed how to handle what lay ahead. Roosevelt was one of the first high schools in the state of Georgia to integrate. Teachers who'd been there for years were handing in their resignations. I had my pick of which grades to teach. I settled on eighth- and ninth-grade English, and also agreed to teach journalism. I had never even taken a journalism course, but serving as coeditor of my high school newspaper was enough of a qualification for Mr. Baxter, the pale, desperate principal who hired me. The loop of my life was about to start over. Maybe I looked on this teaching position as a way to make amends for the pain I'd caused. A kind of penance. Of course, the issues were important to me. Those early years of integration had a courage and a genuineness to them. I felt noble, standing up for these issues. That old sense of rightness kicking in. The idea of being where I should be.

My first morning on the job, police were stationed on all three floors of the school; patrol cars lined the parking lot. I started first-period English reading aloud a story about a teenager who meets the Queen. I then asked my students to name an important person they'd like to meet. A white boy's hand shot up. "I wish I could meet President Kennedy," he said, twisting his pudgy shoulders, glancing around, making sure all eyes were fastened on him. "I'd tell him to get these niggers out of our school!" My eyes immediately took in the room. I *felt* the hush more than I could actually *hear* it. Like a vibration. Did all the children feel this way? I couldn't tell. Such faint, vacant stares. Even the black student, in the front row, his desk inches from where I was standing: a tense blankness. I tried to breathe normally. Tried to think what to say. I said something like this: "Wayne, I'm going to pretend I didn't hear you say that. I'm going to pretend every person in this room wants to live peacefully with our neighbors and we're all going to do our best toward that goal." I remember my response was short. Mainly, because I was having trouble catching my breath.

Weeks later, at the start of homeroom, I heard noises in the coatroom. Scuffling. Murmurings. It was noisy in the classroom, too—children arriving, talking animatedly, laughing, dropping books, scraping chairs. I didn't pay much attention to what might have been heating up in the coatroom. Then: *Maybe I should go check.* I started toward the sounds, got as far as the doorway between the classroom and the coatroom, saw two boys locked tight, struggling against each other—one white, one black, both eighth-graders, both small, shorter than me. Without thinking, I wedged myself in and pushed and pulled at them. "Okay, okay!" I said, using a voice that sounded to my inexperienced self like a voice a teacher might use. I happened to glance down. My loafers and socks were covered in blood. I looked up. That black child's cheek was split wide open, from beneath his eye to the corner of his downturned mouth. He wasn't crying, though. His expression was empty, maybe even helpless, or hopeless. For a second, I couldn't compute. My mind was searching for a narrative to explain. I knew what I was seeing, but I couldn't grasp it. Out of the corner of my eye: the white child's bare little wrist, his hand, the knife he held.

Then, it was a warm afternoon in November, last period of the day, still my first year, journalism class, which was actually the school newspaper staff meeting, with me the faculty sponsor. The editor, a white girl, one of the few who were trying to bring classmates together, began assigning articles. Through the tall, steep windows along one wall, sunlight washed the room. Suddenly, she was interrupted by the static that always preceded an announcement over the loudspeaker. The static seemed to go on longer than usual, as though the whole system might be clearing its throat. Then Mr. Baxter's voice: "Students and teachers of Roosevelt High . . . our president has been shot." Silence. No one in the classroom made eye contact. Suddenly, like an explosion, you could hear students throughout the building, cheering, screaming joyfully, running up and down the halls.

Each incident: staggering. I was seeing firsthand, up close, just how far the state of Georgia had to go. Really, how far the country had to go.

Maybe I was also seeing how far *I* had to go—to

be self-reliant, unconfined, grown up. By the end of my second year teaching, with calm finally settling in at school, I knew I needed a new direction. Atlanta felt like an extension of college. Everyone I knew had attended the University of Georgia, Georgia Tech, or Emory. Time, in some ways, had stopped. I'd always been extremely close to my parents, so tied in; I sensed that with more geographical distance between us, I might emerge. A friend and I decided to move to New York City together. A week before we were to leave, though, she called to say she was getting married instead. I don't think I even uttered the word *congratulations*. I just needed to change her mind: "No, no! We're going to New York! Next week! You and me!" But she was determined. And I flew to LaGuardia alone.

It was late summer 1965. I rented a room at the Barbizon Hotel for Women, an Italian Renaissance building on the Upper East Side, "a safe retreat for career women" (according to the glossy brochure), where men weren't allowed above the ground floor. My room was so small I could lie in bed and open my door at the same time. The day I moved in, I ventured down the hall, knocking on those massive carved doors, introducing myself to each of my neighbors, as any well-bred southerner would do. I can still see the girls' puzzled faces as they cracked their doors half open. And, oh, their anemic greetings. They probably didn't understand a word I was saying.

I landed what I thought was a glamour job at

Filmex, a company that produced TV commercials. But, being the assistant to the production assistant, relieving the switchboard operator at lunch, tending bar and acting friendly to advertising execs when they came to film at the studio turned out not to be glamorous. Just low-paying. I made seventy dollars a week. My brother, Donald, eight years older, who'd lived in New York for years, joked that my paycheck was so small I could cash it on the bus.

I was soon promoted to secretary to Peter Griffith, vice president of Filmex *and* Tippi Hedren's ex-husband *and* Melanie Griffith's father *and* the most gorgeous man I'd ever seen in person. Sometimes his beauty was so startling I had to look away. The biggest problem, though, was that I'd lied about shorthand. When he called me in to his office to take dictation, I wrote down the first letter of each word, then rushed back to my desk to type before I forgot what the letters stood for. Pretty quickly, I was fired.

Next job: secretary to a senior copywriter at Ogilvy & Mather Advertising. This was a lucky break, because my boss knew I wanted to learn copy. He gave me a shot at writing print ads and TV commercials. He submitted my names for new products. I was also taking a copywriting class at The New School. By this time, I had found a roommate and was living in an apartment on East Seventieth between First and Second. I'd lost my heart three times, to Ben, Stuart, and Allen. But my career was now my focus—my love life a little less so.

Nearly two years after landing in New York—it was now late winter 1967—I applied for a copywriting job at Benton & Bowles. As part of my interview, I had to create a new product and an ad campaign to go with it. My invention: the No-Alarm Alarm Clock. You could choose the voice you wanted to hear first thing in the morning—a gentle mother's voice ("Sweetie, time to get up! Breakfast is waiting!"), a sexy somebody ("Hey, babe! Open those eyes and get over here!"), no end to the possibilities for getting you going.

Finally, I made it out of the secretary pool and into my dream job. Two of us—both young female copywriters—were hired at the same time. The vice president of Benton & Bowles told me he was betting on me to "surface first" (his words), and the president was betting on the other new hire. The vice president was young, dimple-chinned, and good-looking; the president was old and white-haired. I felt I'd already won the competition. My days were filled with focus groups, creative sessions with art directors, writing print ads and TV commercials—all for my very own account, Vicks Formula 44 Cough Syrup.

Like the girl in E. B. White's book *Here Is New York*, who moved to Manhattan from a small southern town, I was embracing the city "with the intense excitement of first love," absorbing the city "with the fresh eyes of an adventurer." I was primed for whatever came next.

5

While Henry has the MRI, I sit in the same waiting room I sat in hours ago when he was having the epidural. Only this time there's no one here but me. The lights are dim and there are no sounds. Everything is wrong: Magazines have been left in a mess on tables and chairs. Coffee-stained styrofoam cups and wadded-up tissues are everywhere. It's so quiet. The room can hardly bear the weight of its silence.

Why didn't I bring my cell phone with me? But then, why would I think I'd need it? We were supposed to be here only an hour and a half.

I spot a phone on the reception desk, don't know if patients are allowed to use it, walk over and pick up the receiver. A dial tone! I punch 9 to get out, then dial our son's office. Mike is thirty-four, married, living here in Charlotte. I get his answering machine, hang up, call his house, reach his wife, Brooke, try to explain the sequence of events. Everything comes out jumbled. Next, I call our daughter, Laurie, who's thirty-seven, married, living in Durham. I'm a little better at explaining what has happened, although there is nothing I hate worse than giving my children something to worry about. I would rather haul a great weight for miles than ask them to raise their sweet hands to help. I'm frightened, so frightened, but I hear myself saying *Everything's all right. Everything's going to be all right.*

6

Soon after I started my new job as copywriter, I flew home to Rock Hill to see my parents. My sister and Henry's sister knew each other and wanted to fix Henry and me up on a blind date. I wasn't thrilled to be fixed up. I hadn't brought "dating clothes" with me, and, really, all I'd wanted was to spend some time with my parents. Plus, I'd just started dating a guy from work. I found out later that Henry was just as unthrilled. He told his sister, "I can get my own dates."

But neither of us said no. In fact, our meeting seemed fated.

Days before my trip home, my New York roommate and I had been guests of her aunt and uncle at the Copacabana, where Diana Ross and The Supremes were appearing. Before the show, a fortune-teller made her way around the room, tickled the creases of my palm with her gold-ringed forefinger, got stone still, and, with a wink, said, "You'll soon meet a tall, handsome redhead."

My tall, handsome redhead was born in New York City, grew up in Miami Beach, graduated from the

University of Florida, then optometry school in Chicago. He'd returned home to Miami Beach to join an optometry practice but found it impossible to live with his parents after being on his own for so long. In 1967 he moved to Charlotte to go into practice with another doctor. Months into that job, he quit to open his own office. That's when we met. He was twenty-seven. I was twenty-five.

I hadn't been picked up for a date at my parents' house since high school. I was too old to be single, could see how people in Rock Hill looked at me, *Poor Judy can't get a husband* written all over their faces. I was too old to be opening the front door of my childhood home to a date. Even worse, this particular night Mother was hosting her music club. I'd be bringing somebody I'd never met into the living room and introducing him to my parents—and the entire membership of the Allegro Music Club. I'd feel like Laura in *The Glass Menagerie,* whom everyone was so hoping the "gentleman caller" would fall for. I told Henry to drive to Rock Hill, stop at the first gas station he came to, and call; I'd meet him there.

I asked my sister, Brenda, and her husband, Chuck, who lived in Rock Hill at the time, to drop me off at the Pure Oil station at the corner of Cherry Road and Oakland Avenue. Henry was parked next to a pay phone, across from the gas pumps, waiting for me. Now I felt like a mail-order bride! I slipped out of Brenda and Chuck's car, walked across the asphalt, got into Henry's Volkswagen Beetle, and we took off. It did not occur to Henry or me that maybe he should get out of his car and meet my sister and brother-in-law. At that point, we were both probably thinking *Let's get this over with.*

Eyes on the road, he barely had a chance to look at me, but I got a good look at him. Tall, I was sure over six feet. Red hair—as the fortune-teller had predicted, although I wasn't thinking about this then. Really, his hair was more copper than red. Eyebrows, thick and dark. Big, bull neck and shoulders. He wore a blue short-sleeved oxford-cloth shirt that had obviously been washed and pressed at the dry cleaner. Very neat appearance. *Meticulous.* His arms were furry, golden.

I'd already decided we'd go to the Holiday Inn coffee shop out on the bypass. Rock Hill was not exactly brimming with night spots; our choice was either the Holiday Inn or the Elks Club, where people my parents' age went for prime rib.

Inside the coffee shop, every square little table was set, plates and glasses, silverware and white cloth napkins, as though any minute there'd be a rush of customers. But we were the only ones there. We ordered coffee and talked. And talked. It seemed as though we'd always known one another. At the same time, each new detail about the other's life was a sweet surprise. There was a sunny goodness about this man. And a confidence. He was smart and funny. He not only made me laugh, he laughed at the things I said. And he listened. And asked questions. If I'd been aware of a checklist, every little box would have been inked in.

Our waitress filled. And refilled. Around eleven, the manager ambled over to our table and drawled, "Listen here, folks, I'm closing up, but I'll leave a pot of coffee on, and you can just turn it off when you leave. Close the door behind you. It'll lock by itself."

We stayed till light was rising in the windows.

I don't think we remembered to turn off the coffeepot when we left.

Standing just inside my parents' back door, in the laundry room, beside the washer and dryer and a basket of dirty clothes, we were slowing down with our chatting. I knew what I had to do: I reached up and kissed him good night.

The next day, I told my parents and sister that Henry was the one. I found out later he told his sister the same thing about me.

My dream job was no longer A#1 in importance. Three weeks later, I flew back to the Carolinas to see him.

Friday night we double-dated with Brenda and Chuck at the Pineville Dinner Theater, halfway between Charlotte, where Henry lived, and Rock Hill, where I was staying with my parents. Henry and I were so shining-eyed over each other, we hardly noticed that the rustic barn theater was actually fake rustic, the show was cheesy, and our steaks were tough.

Saturday, I borrowed two bikes from my parents' neighbors, and Henry and I rode out into the country, picnicked on bread and cheese on a blanket in a grassy meadow, talked, made out. Saturday night we saw *Two for the Road,* starring Audrey Hepburn and Albert Finney, a movie that traced the arc of a marriage, from the glorious beginning part to the beginning-to-get-annoyed part. The two of us, light-headed with love, were enthralled with the glorious part.

Then a month of letters back and forth.

Then he drove his Beetle to New York for the weekend.

The most important thing about Friday night, the night he arrived (he was staying with his cousin in The Village, not with me), was that we said the words. *I love you.* He said them first. I blissfully followed.

Saturday night, after Italian food in the neighborhood, we lay side by side in my apartment, on a sofa I'd found on the street. Our conversation was smooth and lazy—when would we see each other again, where would we go from there. It was a conversation that had the future stamped all over it.

I asked what I thought was the logical next question: "Can you picture us growing old together?"

No answer.

I gathered my breath, exhaled, tried to think. Had I ruined everything? Had our relationship just ground to a halt? He still wasn't speaking. Was there any way to reel back my words?

Finally, in a deep-throated voice, he said, "Hmm. That's a loaded question."

Loaded question? We had a lot to talk about.

He said he couldn't afford to get married.

I said don't worry, I can support us.

He said there was the lease he'd signed for his new office.

I said I'd be able to get a good job in Charlotte, coming from a New York ad agency.

He said there was the mammoth loan he'd applied for; he had exactly ninety dollars in his checking account.

I said whatever I needed to say to counteract what he'd just said.

He said he wanted to spend his life with me, but he needed to open his office first, get established, pay back his loan, be able to support me.

I said I wanted to spend my life with him. Beginning now.

The same way I planned to talk myself into a job, I was talking him into marrying me. Such brazenness! As though it were snatched from the air. But when I look back at that night, I know it was the same brazenness I'd found in myself when I broke my engagement, when I taught in a high school roiling with integration, when I moved to New York City alone, when I kissed Henry in the laundry room. The Judy who might seem too timid to take charge—but when she really wants something, she goes after it.

I kept at it until daybreak. Until we got engaged.

•

The next day, before he drove back to Charlotte, he hauled my winter clothes, snow boots, kitchen things, posters from my wall (the same Milton Glaser and Peter Max posters every other young 1960s New Yorker had) out the front door of my apartment, into the elevator, up Seventieth Street to where his car was parked. Then back for more. His pace never slowed. And he never got winded. Nothing was too heavy or too cumbersome. He carried a bottom-heavy coffee table and oversized brass lamp like they were trinkets. As he pulled away from the curb and sailed off down Second Avenue—that tiny Volkswagen swollen to fullness—I stood there, waving, feeling a stunning happiness.

The next day I quit my job at Benton & Bowles. It was June 1967. I sold my share in a Fire Island summer rental, packed my things, moved back home to Rock Hill to be close to Henry, just twenty-six miles away, in Charlotte. We began planning our wedding.

Eight weeks after we'd gotten engaged—August 20, 1967—we were married at my parents' house. Our two-o'clock ceremony took place at two-thirty. (I didn't know then that Henry is always late. He arrived at two-fifteen, perfectly relaxed, not even aware he'd shown up after our guests. I noticed, but was so madly in love, I didn't care.) My father gave me away, which meant he walked me from my old bedroom down the hall into the living room, where Parrish's Flowerland had set up an orchid- and ivy-covered chuppah. Our twenty-eight guests—aunts, uncles, cousins, two friends for him, one for me—sat in chairs lining the room. When the rabbi began, everyone stood. Henry and I never took our eyes off each other. His face was flushed, my heart was pounding, we said our vows.

After the ceremony, we had lunch at long tables set up on the screened porch. A perfectly calibrated afternoon pulling the two of us along. Henry and I stayed later than anyone thought we should, because we didn't want it to end—all that sweet equilibrium, everything as it should be, everything still to come. We were happy beyond our wildest dreams.

Early evening, I changed into my going-away outfit: a red linen sheath with navy-blue trim, navy-blue patent-leather heels and matching purse, short white cotton gloves. We ran down the front steps of my parents' house in a snow of rice, drove to Charlotte, stopped at Riccio's for takeout pepperoni pizza, and spent our first night in Henry's furnished one-bedroom bachelor apartment, which would be our home that first year.

We called it love. I felt familiar to him, he felt familiar to me: We were so much alike, there was a rush of recognition. A humming. Right away, we trusted each other. At the same time, a key part of our mutual attraction was that we were so opposite. He completed me; I completed him. What I lacked, he had, what he lacked, I had, puzzle piece to puzzle piece. As though we were bringing each other into being. That incredibly delicate meeting place where two people come together to construct one life.

We'd waited until that first night for sex. Those

warm, astonishing longings had definitely played a part in our swift push toward marriage. In a few short years, because of the pill, couples would meet, have sex, marry, or not marry. We were part of that last generation of couples who got married in order to have sex. But, really, who can explain love? Lust? And who can tell the difference?

The next day we flew to Dorado Beach, Puerto Rico, for our honeymoon. Every morning, on our own private balcony, we ate pancakes and sipped coffee and watched tiny yellow birds swoop in to perch, precariously, on the edge of our plates.

7

After the MRI, our same nurse leads me back down the long hall to our same tiny, bare holding room in the outpatient clinic. Neither of us is saying a word. It's almost evening. Before I have a chance to sit down, Henry is wheeled back in. He's sound asleep. Demerol obviously working. *Good. He's out of pain.* I move a chair closer to him to wait for the MRI results. When I sit down, I realize how shaky my legs are, how unreliable. But I don't know this until I'm no longer depending on them to hold me up.

·

The physiatrist knocks on the door and enters the room, all one motion. He brings a whoosh of air in with him. Or maybe it's just the sound of the heavy door pushing wide open. He reports that the head of radiology read the scan and found nothing significant. I don't know what to make of this. My husband is paralyzed—and the radiologist sees nothing significant? I look over at Henry to gauge his reaction, to see how we're going to handle this, what we'll do next. I need him to react. Now. But that's not going to happen. He's still sleeping. His jaw is loose; his mouth hangs open, as if any minute he *could* say something, weigh in, take charge.

The physiatrist is now repeating the same sentence, over and over: "I've given seven thousand of these, and this has never happened!" He's intense, overkeen. All nervous energy. "I've given seven thousand of these and this has never happened!

"Maybe," he says, changing gears, still agitated, "the nurse switched the vials. Maybe your husband was given five cc's of bupivacaine and two cc's of saline, instead of the other way around. Maybe I injected a Tarlov cyst. Maybe I penetrated an artery. I mean, the artery of Adamkiewicz. Maybe your husband's anatomy is different from other people's and the anomaly is what caused the . . ."

What's a Tarlov cyst? An artery of Adamkiewicz? What is he saying?

There's a frantic quality to his conjecturing. So much emotion in his voice that it sounds brittle. I can't identify the emotion. But it's making the air feel thin. I want to take in a gulp of air, but I can barely breathe. I don't answer. He doesn't notice. He's filling in every sliver of silence, injecting each small space with words.

8

Henry and I have always been talkers. We never run out of things to say to each other.

After turkey sandwiches at the kitchen table, Mother said she had some advice for us, now that we were married. It had been about five months since the wedding. She was settling in to my father's big upholstered chair in their living room, reaching across the end table for her Salems and lighter. My father had come home to eat with us but was now back at work. (He owned two clothing stores on Main Street—The Smart Shop and King's Men's Shop.) Henry and I sat on the sofa, across from Mother, my shoulder tight against his upper arm, his leg pressed against mine. We were so young, so crazy in love, we were probably eager to hear her advice. We believed deeply in "us"; I'm sure we thought we were already doing whatever she was going to tell us we should be doing.

She blew smoke out of the side of her mouth, almost over her shoulder, to keep it from drifting toward our faces. Her words went something like this: "You have to keep talking. Keep communicating. Talking is what gets you through, to the other side. There shouldn't be anything you can't discuss." I could imitate the way she smoked—two graceful fingers holding the cigarette, thumb holding the smaller two fingers back. "Put all your eggs in the communication basket."

Oh, and one more bit of advice: "Never buy a king-sized bed." She may have taken a drag at that moment, creating a small space, a few seconds for her words to sink in. She finished with *why* we should never buy a king-sized bed: "You could go the whole night without touching."

Over the coming years, we would have a plain mattress and box spring, a table-hard Tempur-Pedic, then back to a mattress and box spring. We'd add a pillow top. We'd try no-iron polyester sheets, one hundred percent cotton, sateen, bamboo. But we would never have a king-sized bed. I have to say, though, sometimes I'd wonder about a bigger bed when we both were deep in sleep and he'd turn to face me, flop really close, then begin snoring.

·

Henry's and my favorite romantic movie has always been *Two for the Road*. Maybe because we saw it on our second date. Maybe because when we saw it again, years later, we finally focused on the whole movie, the whole marriage.

The dialogue Henry and I love to quote:

Albert Finney: "What kind of people just sit in a restaurant and don't say one word to each other?"

Audrey Hepburn: "Married people."

Of course, newlywed passion is not sustainable. We reward the person who means the most to us with our boredom, having settled quietly into ourselves, accepting the distance that inevitably encroaches between husband and wife.

Early in our marriage, Henry called me over to the TV to show me the #1 NBA draft pick. He explained in detail why this guy was picked first, why he (no more than a kid, really, albeit a tall kid with big hands) was so much better than the second pick. I asked questions—what college he attended, which NBA team Henry had thought would get him. Henry filled in. I joined him on the couch to hear more.

Years into our marriage, he would call me over to see the NBA picks. I'd let him know by a slight mouth twitch that he was interrupting me. I would secretly wonder what it would be like to be married to a man who was a writer like me, someone who was as indifferent to sports as I am, who would call me over to read a line from a poem.

Here's what I believe Audrey Hepburn and Albert Finney were trying to say in their silence: *This marriage isn't perfect, but there's something about our love for each other that is.*

·

My aunt Katie, Mother's younger sister, once told me that when she and Uncle Irwin ate in a restaurant, she didn't want the two of them to look like an old married couple who had run out of things to say to each other. She came up with this strategy:

She'd gaze up at him, devotedly, and whisper, "A-B-C."

He knew to answer in a hushed voice only the two of them could hear: "D-E-F-G-H." People in the restaurant would see a man and a woman deeply engaged in intimate conversation.

"I-J?" she would inquire, delicately.

"K and L and M and N and O" was his usual answer.

9

Henry and I are alone again. He's still sleeping. Every now and then his eyelids flicker and blink open. For a startled moment, he doesn't seem to know where he is. I touch his face, so that my fingertips can refresh his memory. He's groggy. Keeps blinking. He's about to doze off again. Before he does, I flip the sheet over and run my hand down each of his legs.

"Can you feel me touching you?"

"No," he whispers.

I cover him up. He goes back to sleep. His little snores lull me into pretending, just for this minute, that everything is okay and he's just resting after a very successful epidural and soon I'll leave to get the car and he'll be waiting for me at the front door of the clinic, upright, free from pain, ready to go home.

It occurs to me that I should start writing everything down that has happened. I find an old grocery list in my handbag, turn it over in my palm, begin to write, starting with arriving at the clinic this afternoon. I decide the paper is too small, wad it up, stuff it back into my handbag. I pull a paper towel from the wall dispenser, rest it on the over-the-bed table, the kind you see in hospital rooms, this one pushed into the corner, a stool underneath. I'm standing and leaning over the table, but instead of recording the sequence of events, I start scribbling words I would never say out loud. *WHAT THE FUCK IS GOING ON?! SHIT! CRAP! HELLFIRE!* I like the coarseness of the paper towel. It feels right. I keep scribbling, bearing down hard, my ballpoint pen ripping the paper. *WHAT THE FUCK IS GOING ON?! SHIT! CRAP! HELL-FIRE!* I realize I'm clenching my teeth. As though I'm gnawing through misery.

But wait. Take a breath. Get a grip.

I pull another paper towel from the wall, roll the stool out from under the table, sit, use the table for my desk, begin to record the events of this day, listing them as though they have their own logical order. I start with today's date: March 24, 2006.

.

I've always written. I began writing poems in the third grade, started keeping a diary that same year, kept a diary every year until college, filling each page, top to bottom, January 1 through December 31. After I got married, I wrote in journals. And, of course, my work involved writing: copywriter for a Charlotte ad agency. Just before I gave birth to Laurie, I left that job and started freelancing ad copy, stayed with that for years. I wrote book reviews for newspapers, commentaries for public radio, essays for a local arts and entertainment weekly. I wrote two poetry collections, two novels, a memoir.

I grew up in a family that relied on writing down words. I still have the beautifully crafted letters my father wrote in his scalloped script at important junctures in my life—when I'd won something I'd worked hard for, when I didn't win, when I was facing tough decisions, when I thought I'd made the wrong decision. I can picture my mother at her desk in their bedroom, writing long letters to her two sisters, nodding as she went, spilling every detail of our family's lives. After she died, when Brenda and I were clearing out our parents' house, getting it ready to sell, I found a diary Mother had kept in 1929, 1930, 1931. It had fallen behind a row of books on the living room shelves. In 1931 she was dating my father. I'd never even known the diary existed. All those exclamation points. Page after page: "Gee, Diary!!!" That leather-bound book and its buoyant moments had probably long been forgotten in the cloud of her Alzheimer's.

·

Now I'm chronicling everything that's going on because I'm hoping the concrete details will help me help Henry. If I gather enough facts, if I can *see* the facts, I'll be able to fix what's wrong. If I lay the events out on paper, in sequence, then I can add them up like a row of numbers, and the right answer will pop out.

An hour passes. Maybe a half hour. Maybe only minutes. I'm aware of each rough tick of the clock on the wall, like somebody tapping on the window, wanting to come in. But I'm finding it hard to keep track of how much time is actually passing.

Henry rouses and I reach under to rub, just below his waist, on the left side. He says he can feel my touch. My jaw, which I realize has been locked with strain, relaxes a little. Maybe, just maybe, the doctor was right and he'll be fine. It'll just take time. I write this down.

Another hour or so, and I run my hand over his hips, on both sides. "I can feel your hand here. On my left hip," he says, eyes half closed. This, too, I record.

Later he drifts awake again and I touch his left thigh. "Yes, I can feel it," he says, with a hint of his normal energy.

I almost sing my response. "Oh, good! Good! See?" Like a child's tune that can reassure both of us.

Little by little, hour by hour, feeling on his left side seems to be traveling from his waist down to his thigh, to his knee, to his shin. As though his left side is trying to show his right side what it needs to do. But the returned sensation on the left is uneven—not the entire left side. Some places are still numb. And all feeling stops just above where a sock would come up to.

There is still no feeling at all on his right side, from his waist down to his toes.

One of the nurses who has been checking on us periodically motions me out into the hall, pats my forearm, says she used to work in anesthesiology, she's seen this before, he'll be fine. I want to believe her. Yes. He'll be fine. Of course, she's right. She's young and pretty and her straight, white teeth are beautiful when she smiles, so surely I can trust what she's saying.

We're down to her and one other nurse. Everyone else has gone home for the night.

Now what? Do we stay here, in this clinic? Do I take him home? What's the plan?

10

Friday night, months into our marriage, after catching the eleven-o'clock weather on TV—snow, lots of snow, in the North Carolina mountains—Henry and I decided to go skiing early the next morning. A two-hour drive from Charlotte to Beech Mountain.

During the years I'd lived in New York, I had taken the train to Vermont several times to ski with friends. I'd signed up for lessons, bought a cute ski outfit, learned to snowplow, practiced, never really became expert, was just good enough. Henry had never skied.

·

After we rented skis, boots, and poles, we got ourselves bundled up and stepped out into the frigid Appalachian morning. I was wearing my burgundy-and-white down jacket and matching burgundy ski pants. Henry was wearing stretched-out jeans and the tan, permanently stained windbreaker he'd had since high school.

"Let's take a lesson together," I said, billows of vapor smoking from my mouth.

"Nah," he said, stamping his skis down hard, one, then the other, as though he'd grown up wearing snow skis in Miami Beach. "We don't really need a lesson. Let's just mess around, get our bearings. How hard could it be?"

.

The sun was rising by slow degrees. We hopped onto the beginners' chairlift, lowered the bar across our laps, began our ride up the mountain.

"This is great!" he said, with that old familiar readiness for adventure.

"Well, before you even think about skiing down this mountain, I need to teach you how to snowplow. When we get off the lift, just wait. I'll show you."

The chairlift was nearing the top. We could see skiers ahead of us on the lift raising their bars, sliding out of their chairs, skiing smoothly off to the side. Henry must have had a sudden realization that the lift was not going to actually come to a stop, that he'd have to jump off. Which he did. But he jumped *before* we got to the jumping-off place. The ground was far below. Half in the chair, half out, he was thrown completely off balance, one leg hanging way down, the other leg kicking out toward me. He tried to right himself, flung his arms out, poles jabbing, swinging in all directions, which knocked me completely out of the chair. He somehow landed on his feet. I landed on my back, off to the side, deep in unplowed, crusty snow.

We were both laughing so hard, it took him forever to excavate me. His skis kept crossing. His poles were banging around. And where were *my* poles? And how would I get my own skis untwisted?

But finally we were put back together again, standing at the top of the slope, taking in the scene. It was swarming with skiers.

Then I sensed this sudden activity beside me. Henry was digging in his poles, leaning forward in a racing position, leaning *so* far forward that he was half kneeling—and now he was pushing himself off!

"Wait!" I yelled. "You don't know how to stop!"

He zipped through the first cluster of skiers, veered sharply to one side, dangerously close to the snow machine, which was shooting out mountains of snowy clouds, turning everything shadowy. Then he zigzagged to the other side, just past a woman who was taking it nice and slow with a little girl skiing between her legs. Henry barely missed them. He was picking up more and more speed, his skis pointed straight down the mountain, going faster and faster— all the way to the bottom, to the end of the trail, where it lolled flat.

But. He *kept going.*

Past where the trail ended.

Onto the patchy grass. *Beyond* the grass. Where

his skis stuck deep in mud. He didn't exactly fall. He just allowed his body to fold gently into the horizon.

Then he swiveled around to squint up at me. His face, in that moment, appeared lit by the sun. It was obvious he considered his first run a tremendous success. Exactly what it should have been.

He told me he wanted to "mess around" some more, try to figure it out. I spent the morning in ski school. It had been at least a year since I'd skied and I wanted to review the basics, make sure my form was right, just generally go over everything. By the time my lesson was done and I was ready for any beginner slope on the mountain, Henry had taken off for the expert runs.

11

Beautiful-smile nurse tells us Henry is about to be transferred to a room in the hospital. Since the outpatient clinic adjoins the hospital, we won't have to venture out into the dark.

I follow behind the gurney, through long connecting passageways, stillness overwhelming everything.

And then we enter the hospital. That subterranean hospital smell, I can almost feel it on my tongue. The sudden dilated brightness and activity—this late at night!—hurts my eyes and ears.

The transporter and Henry continue on to a room. I head in the opposite direction to Admitting.

By the time I get to the room, Henry is hooked up to an IV. A nurse is adjusting the drip. Her hair is halfway gray. Her voice is quiet and southern when she explains that the doctor ordered intravenous steroids to reduce any swelling that might have occurred in my husband's spinal cord.

I thank her, tell her that sounds like a good thing to do.

The room is spotless, floor shiny, trash can empty,

crisp plastic bag folded over the edge. No evidence of any patient ever having been here before us. Just as I'm beginning to lose myself in the details of where we are, the phone on the bedside table rings. It's a jolt, not just because of the lusty sound, but also because it feels so odd for a phone to ring in this room, at this time. As though we're already living here. We've never seen this room before in our lives and, just like that, we've set up residence to such an extent that someone is calling us.

It's Mike, our son. I report to him all that has gone on, trying to sound optimistic, using my bravest voice. He knows me well, though, and says he'll come right away. I know him well, too, and hear the fright in his voice. I tell him not to come, his dad's resting, mostly sleeping, I'll either spend the night or go home soon, he can come in the morning. He has spoken with Laurie, who's driving in from Durham early tomorrow. What I most want is for both of them to be standing beside me this minute. But I know not to give in to that scared part of me.

Instead, I act as though I have a starring role in a play. The calm wife and mother. Who, even though an unfortunate accident has occurred and no one seems to know the way forward, remains stoic with her family, remains gracious and polite to the hospital staff.

My mother is really something, Mike will say to Brooke after he hangs up the phone.

Isn't it amazing she's so calm? our nurse will whisper to another nurse.

And so nice, the other nurse will say.

And then the grown children of the patient will come to the hospital. *What a lovely family,* the nurses will say. *You'd think at least one of them would be pitching a fit, demanding answers. But no, they're all so composed. And nice.*

.

Around midnight, the question has to be dealt with: Will I spend the night?

"Go, go," Henry says. "I'll be fine. I'll just sleep. You need to get some rest."

"But what if you need me?" I turn his left wrist to check his IV. "What if there are decisions to be made?" I smooth the hem of the sheet back over his blanket. "I think I should stay, just in case."

"If I need something, I'll ring for the nurse." The fingers of his right hand crawl up the mattress above his left shoulder. They find the call button, slide it down, closer in. "Nobody's going to be making any decisions in the middle of the night. Go home, sweetie. I'll see you in the morning."

I kiss him good night, still unsure whether to leave or not, whether to be hopeful or prepare myself for something life-rattling.

We should have left for home—together—nine hours ago.

.

I flick on the answering machine in the kitchen. While I'm listening to messages from friends and family—how did the news travel so fast?—I glance at our lunch plates and glasses left on the counter. Those ham-and-cheese sandwiches seem as long ago as our wedding lunch.

When I finally roll back the comforter, it's Henry's side I sleep on. He always kids me that, although he knows which is his side regardless of where we're sleeping (in a motel, at a friend's house, even camping in a tent), I never know. There's something wrong with my spatial relations. Which means I also have trouble judging which Tupperware container is the right size for which glob of leftovers. I try one after the other before I finally hit it right, ending up with a million containers on the counter, all needing to be washed. Am I choosing Henry's side because it's next to the phone and I can catch it quickly if he needs me? Or because the pillow still holds the imprint, and the cotton still holds the smell, of his cheek?

12

We were lying in bed, lights out, in our apartment on Abbey Place. Married maybe nine months, we were planning the future, the way newlyweds do. A whole sweet life waiting. Suddenly, Henry raised himself up on his elbow, his eyes shiny in the dark.

"If only I hadn't screwed around so much my freshman and sophomore years in college," he said. "I would've had the grades to apply to medical school."

He had changed the subject, or so it seemed at first, although, really, he was just looking into the future and not liking what he saw there. What he saw were the constraints of his profession.

I envied his screwing around in college. Even though I'd attended what was known as *the* party school of the South, maybe of the entire country, I was a serious student with a deep and abiding faith in term papers, studying, exams. Of the three children in my family, I was the most committed. But by the time it was my turn to apply to college, my parents were older, maybe tired, no longer believed that where you went was such a critical decision, especially since they hadn't been able to talk my brother or sister into applying to top schools. They'd wanted Donald to attend an Ivy League school. He chose the University of North Carolina. An excellent school, just not what my parents had in mind. They'd wanted Brenda to attend Sarah Lawrence or Wellesley. She chose the University of Georgia, also a reasonable choice, since it had a highly regarded art department and she was an art major. I picked Georgia because—well, Brenda had gone there, and it felt safe and familiar.

Once I was a student at Georgia, though, I realized it was not the right school for me. I hated that it was impossible to flunk out, hated that you could make D's and stay forever. But it never occurred to me to transfer. I thought you made your choice and stayed put. I spent four years forming committee after committee to transform the school into a more academic place. If I tried hard enough, I could turn the University of Georgia into MIT. I threw myself into extracurriculars, campus politics, made Dean's List, Who's Who, Mortar Board (the highest national honorary on campus, for scholarship, leadership, and service).

But now I was wishing I'd experienced college the way Henry had, partied more, been less dedicated, more reckless.

Because Henry had not been *achieving up to his potential* (words that appeared frequently on his report cards), his parents (really, his disciplinarian mother) sent him to Riverside Military Academy for his last two and a half years of high school. He hated military school. But he graduated third in his class. His first day at the University of Florida, he asked his resident adviser, "What time do I have to be in at night?" The answer: "You don't have to be in. At all." That was it. He had missed out on all that adolescent dating, drinking, partying, making his own decisions—and now it was time for all four. Good-bye, strict mother. So long, military school. He spent his textbook money on beer. Never bought a book. By the end of his sophomore year, he was sleeping with his girlfriend, his grades had plummeted, and he'd received a probation letter.

Junior year, he moved out of the fraternity house, into an apartment, and started studying. He made straight A's. But it was too late. Because his freshman and sophomore grades had been so low, optometry school seemed his only option for a medical career. There, he did very well. After graduation, he passed every optometric board he took. Ten years into his practice, he would be accepted as a Fellow of the American Academy of Optometry. But now he wished he could have become an ophthalmologist, an eye surgeon. He wanted to do more than examine eyes and fit contact lenses.

"You could still go to medical school," I said. "I can support us. We don't have children. It's a perfect time."

Even in the dark, I could see him pressing his lips together, that flinty expression on his face. "No, it's too late," he said. "I'm twenty-eight. I couldn't do it then. I can't do it now."

"Of course you can do it now. What's stopping you? Think you're too old? Ancient at twenty-eight?" I was surprised at the edge of impatience in my voice.

"Maybe making a living is stopping me. Maybe the office space I've leased. Maybe the loan I have to pay off." I wasn't surprised at the edge in his voice, considering the edge in mine. What was surprising was that he was *raising* his voice, when I was inches away, my pillow touching his pillow.

Our first big fight.

"As though those are the real reasons!" I didn't raise my voice. But I did add more edge. "The *real* reason is you're stubborn!"

"You're the one who's stubborn! I think I know how I feel about this subject!" Was he yelling?

"Okay, I take it back. You're not stubborn. You just have no vision." I still was not yelling. Just attacking his character.

"You are *so bossy*!" Now he was yelling *and* attacking my character. He was so mad his face looked like it could crack. "Why don't you just relax!" he said.

"I hate when somebody tells me to relax."

And so it went, a gradual breaking apart.

Which is how all our arguments in the future would go: He would yell. I'd get sarcastic. We'd stop speaking.

The next morning we brushed our teeth, got on

our clothes, grabbed breakfast, left for work without saying good morning, without looking at each other. We were both furious over having married someone who wouldn't see things the right way. After work, we went out for pizza and didn't say a word the entire meal. We just sat there, Charlotte's own Audrey Hepburn and Albert Finney.

Because we'd gotten married so soon after we'd met, we had never really seen the other's style of fighting. My icy cool was new to him, the way I acted as though everything was fine, yet mean words were slipping out of my mouth. His temper was new to me. I'd never heard anyone yell at someone they loved. Really, I had no idea married couples even fought. *We're headed for divorce,* I thought. My parents had never argued in front of my brother, sister, and me— my mother's idea, since her parents had battled endlessly and she was determined that her own household be calm and peaceful. Our home was *so* calm and peaceful, aunts and uncles stayed with us when they were recuperating from surgery. "Kurtz Rest Home" was our joke name among our relatives.

While all that peace and calm gave Donald, Brenda, and me a sanctuary of a childhood, it did not prepare us for the realities of marriage. Brenda told me that the first time she and Chuck had an argument, she was certain their marriage was over. Donald *never* learned to work things out. Before he got married and after his divorce, he had a string of girlfriends. Women were always attracted to him. But at the first sign of conflict, he would say to himself, *What do I need this shit for?* And with stunning swiftness, he was out of there.

Henry's home life had been explosive. Both his parents possessed hot tempers. Their fights were frequent, loud, and intense. He entered into our marriage ready for the first round.

We both had a lot to learn.

·

For years after our big discussion about med school, I believed I was right and he was wrong. That he *could* have changed course. And we would have managed. And he would've been engaged in a career that felt more challenging and fulfilling. He did take pleasure in parts of optometry: the interaction with his patients, mainly. He also liked not being on call, liked setting his own schedule, spending as much time as he wanted with patients, being able to take off to be with his family. And when North Carolina passed a law allowing optometrists to diagnose eye disease and prescribe medication, work became more interesting to him.

But was that decision really as crucial as it felt back then? Time after time, we neglect one path in favor of another. We go straight instead of turning. Looking back, who can say one way would have been better than another? The questions rise and fall. Our lives play out.

13

The morning after the epidural, around eight, I arrive at the hospital. As I enter Henry's room, I see that his covers are twisted into a knot on the side of the bed. His cotton gown is pushed up in thick folds under his chin. For a second, I take in his broad, hairy chest. But then my eyes clamp onto the nurse's hands. She is easing a thin rubber tube farther and farther into his penis. Henry is tapping the mattress with his index finger, a small gesture he thinks no one can see but which tells me how much it hurts, even though he's not about to say so.

"What's going on?" I ask the nurse, aware that there are many different inflections I could use, but I'm choosing this neutral one. At least, until I find out more. I'm determined to behave well. Hold on to my manners.

She holds up one finger to let me know she'll answer in a minute. I smile in response, letting her know I'm fine waiting. We're acting like we're best friends.

Is it possible the other catheter slipped out? Did it stop working? Do catheters need to be replaced every day? I'm testing different explanations in my mind. Henry is not letting up with the tapping. I lean down and press my face, still cool from the spare March morning, to his sweaty, determined face.

"Apparently, the physiatrist called in late last night," he says in a voice that sounds breathy, gravelly, "and he left orders for my catheter to be removed. I think it was around five this morning when they took it out. But I couldn't pee. I'm getting all these IV fluids and my bladder is very full. They have to catheterize me again."

Why did they expect him to be able to pee when he's paralyzed on one side? I should have gotten here earlier. I could have prevented them from removing the catheter. I should've spent the night. Why did I let him talk me into leaving?

This calm, polite wife is suddenly ragged with fear. And anger. *What were they thinking to remove the catheter?* I look at the nurse with my most irritated face, keep looking at her to make sure she sees I'm no longer smiling, that I'm really, really mad now. I understand that it was the doctor's orders, not hers. But I don't care. She's the one who's catheterizing him. She's the one I'm mad at.

Now every decision feels weighted. I'm terrified of deciding wrong, allowing someone *else* to decide wrong, making a mess. I just can't end up feeling we should have taken a right turn instead of a left, should have neglected one path in favor of another. There ought to be a course in school for this sort of thing. Calamity 101. I wish I could do everything in life twice. It's not until the second time that I begin to catch on.

14

This afternoon Henry is transferred by EMS to another hospital in Charlotte. The one you go to when your condition is serious. The sensory and motor nerve function in his left leg is spotty and stops just above his ankle. He still can't feel or move his right leg. At all.

In his new room, he has a grab bar above his bed, which means he can change his position in the bed. I tell him he's lucky to have such good upper-body strength.

A transporter arrives to take him down for his second MRI, with and without contrast dye. The transporter has brought an aide with him. Both men are young and muscular. Mike arrives at the same time they're expertly using the sheet on the bed like a sling—"one, two, three, now!"—to slide Henry over to the gurney.

Mike is six feet, about the same height as Henry, but slimmer. His khakis and button-down are pressed; he always looks great in his clothes. He reminds me of the characters Tom Hanks plays, how decent they always are. Mike gives Henry a kiss on the forehead. I love this about our son, that he's never too old—never too much of a grown man—to show affection. I also love his empathetic nature, the way he can understand a person or a situation and respond with a kind heart. He's in finance, a partner in his own firm. With his aptitude for economics and his love of sports, he's like Henry. But in most other ways, he's like me. Sometimes our similarities are so far-reaching, they take us by surprise. For example, he's as lacking in spatial relations as I am. The only puzzle I've ever been good at is the one he and Laurie had when they were really young. It was one of those thick wooden things that consisted of a banana, an apple, an orange, and grapes. Each piece had a little knob. That might have been the last puzzle Mike could work, also.

The two of us follow the gurney down the hall, into the elevator, down another hall to Imaging. The transporter and Henry go one way, Mike and I the other.

We wait in the Imaging waiting room. I fill him in on everything. When it hurts too much to rehash, I ask about Tess, his one-year-old daughter. He tells funny stories. I want to be distracted.

.

Finally, our same physiatrist comes out. Something inside me is coming loose and fluttering. I force myself to ease my shoulders back down. Mike and I both stand to greet him. He's tall and good-looking, like Mike. The two men stand eye to eye. I'm glad Mike is tall. Am I thinking of Mike as a substitute bodyguard, here to take his father's place, temporarily, until Henry can take over again?

The physiatrist holds up two sheets of paper and says, "The neuroradiologist who read your husband's films and I went online and found this report on paraplegia after lumbosacral nerve root blocks." He shuffles the two pages, manages to slide the first sheet behind the second sheet, hands them both to me, and points to the last paragraph on page two. Mike reads over my shoulder:

CONCLUSIONS: We present the cases of three patients who had lasting paraplegia or paraparesis after the performance of a nerve root block. We propose that the mechanism for this rare but devastating complication is the concurrence of two uncommon circumstances, the presence of an unusually low origin of the artery of Adamkiewicz and an undetected intraarterial penetration of the procedure needle.

It's hard for me to concentrate, to take in such unfamiliar words. But, *lasting paraplegia.* Those two words are clear and straightforward. I understand exactly what they mean. This paralysis is not going away.

The physiatrist is saying that the neuroradiologist who just read Henry's films had actually *been at the same hospital*—New York Hospital!—where those three "events" took place! He was even there *when they occurred*—isn't that *amazing*? What are the chances of *that* happening?

Adrenalized. That's the word I would use to describe the physiatrist.

He says the computer printout is mine to keep. He ran it off for me.

Is it that he's intrigued at his involvement in such a rare and exotic case? Or is he simply relieved to find a precedent for what happened? Either way, his focus is on himself. I want his focus on Henry.

He goes back to saying, "I've given seven thousand of these and this has never happened! I've given seven thousand of these and this has never happened!"

Why isn't he saying he's *sorry* this happened? Why isn't he sympathizing? Why isn't he rerouting all that energy into trying to find a solution?

"Please don't keep saying that," I say stiffly, feeling my cheeks go pink. "It's just not helpful."

My muscles ache from holding myself back from saying more—angry words I might regret. After all, we still need him to guide us through.

I don't know whether he reacts or not. I can't look up. My eyes are on the papers I'm holding in my trembling hands. Those words: *lasting paraplegia.*

Mike does not ask a single question. I don't, either.

The physiatrist shakes hands with Mike, pats my

elbow because he can see I'm working too hard to hold on to these papers to even attempt to shake anybody's hand. He says he's leaving for vacation today. It's his child's spring break, and he and his family are going away for a week.

15

We'd been married seven years when Henry learned to fly a plane. He envisioned the two of us flitting here and there for quick vacations, we'd have stylish luggage with souvenir travel stickers, the wind would blow our hair on the tarmac, we'd take our children along, the whole family lifting our wings and rising above the clouds.

But first he needed to take me up. I was not eager. I kept putting it off. Not quite nervy enough to say no—afraid to fly in a small plane, but not wanting to hurt his feelings—I kept postponing.

Finally, on a windless, blue-sky day, I said okay. He wanted us to fly to Gastonia, twenty-two miles West of Charlotte. The flight would be short, easy, just enough for me to see how much fun flying with him could be.

Fun is not the word I would have used to describe the experience. I did *not* think it was fun closing my own door; it felt so "unofficial." Where was the flight attendant? I'd never closed an airplane door before;

what if I closed it wrong and it flapped open during takeoff?

As soon as we were aloft, Henry started pointing out the sights, proudly, as though he'd put each one in that exact spot for my entertainment.

"See Carowinds?" he exclaimed happily, yelling over the vibration of the plane and the nonstop staticky instructions spewing from the radio. "And the river? See? Over there?" He was probably thinking: *This is everything.*

I was thinking what if he missed something important while he was showing me the Catawba River. I certainly couldn't hear what the control tower was saying. Could he? "Are you listening?" I pointed at the radio. "You need to be paying attention!"

What if something happened to him and it was up to me to get the plane down? Laurie was five, Mike two—what if we crashed and left them orphans? I could easily see Henry slumped over, unconscious, and me frantically radioing the control tower, and some guy trying to talk me through landing the plane. *Okay, Mrs. Goldman, do you see the instrument panel?*

The flight, it turned out, was as smooth as ribbon. The landing precise and perfect.

"Well?" Henry said. "How'd you like it?"

"I'm thinking I'll take the bus home" was my answer, purse under my arm, tight against my side.

I didn't take the bus. I stayed right there in the copilot's seat, beside my husband, who remained healthy and conscious as he flew us through that majestic open sky, safely back home.

But I never flew with him again.

And then: a near-accident. He had promised to be home by six and it was already after six. He needed to get the plane down quickly. (Of course, this was totally normal for Henry. He thinks if we're invited to somebody's house for dinner at seven, he should start getting ready at seven. Whatever he's doing at the moment is the most important thing in the world. He's never ready to move to what's next.)

His landing, this time, did not go perfectly. The runway was too short, his speed too great, no way he could bring it down. At the last minute, he aborted the landing and put everything he had into lifting the plane. But the flaps were out all the way and he couldn't get enough altitude. Up, up, up. Still, it was not rising fast enough. He could see the telephone wires just beyond the end of the runway. They were coming closer and closer. Wires thin as grass were growing thicker and blacker.

His plane cleared those wires by inches.

That's when he realized if he was going to continue flying, he needed to fly more, keep his skills fine-tuned. It did not appear—to either of us—that I would be joining him. Flying alone meant he would spend a lot of time away from his family. He didn't want that.

Even though I kept seeing myself as the small, spineless wife of a big, strong man, I was actually asserting myself all over the place. I can't remember if my refusal to join him led to arguments. I can't imagine it didn't. My selfishness, my lack of sensitivity in seeing things from his perspective, was not noble, even as I was insisting that I was right. He must have tried to persuade me otherwise. He must have felt pretty exasperated. Of course, he knew I was a worrier. And he wasn't the type of husband who would want his wife to fly if she were afraid. But this was an instance in which *my* fear dictated *his* choices.

The give and take in a marriage.

He loved to fly. I didn't. So he gave up flying.

Maybe not so much give and take. Maybe just him giving and me taking.

16

Mike and I take the elevator up to the room. We're not talking about his daughter, Tess, anymore. We're not talking at all.

Laurie has arrived and is sitting beside Henry's bed, holding his hand. The two of them are in mid-conversation. She's so much like her father—both generous, neither likes to say no to anyone or anything. Both have an openness about them. They're optimistic, energetic, never tired, don't need sleep.

But our normally exuberant daughter does not look so exuberant. She raises her chin when Mike and I enter. I see her green eyes, the thick tangle of reddish-brown curls framing that pretty, fine-featured face. Henry used to tease her that he didn't understand how she managed to breathe through such a tiny nose. And, for a flash of a second, I see her as a child, age three, meticulously writing her name, leaning back, cocking that busy little head of hers, then adding two more lines to the capital *E* at the end of her name because, to her eye, to this future graphic designer to whom patterns and exquisite detail will always matter, an *E* with five short lines looks better than an *E* with its usual three. I look at her in this room of white sheets and flexible straws and glaring lightbulbs and see that she is not doing a good job at all of hiding a fretwork of worry.

Mike and I tell them what we now know and give them the printout. Laurie holds it, leaning close to Henry. They read it together, silently. I think they're both shaking their heads, but I can't tell for sure. Do they see those words, *lasting paraplegia?*

17

A 1975 photo: Henry is sitting on the loveseat in his sister Ruth's den. Sun-tanned and laughing—those brown eyes and dark, shaggy brows—he's wearing jeans and a soft, light-colored denim shirt, sleeves rolled up. Laurie, six years old and laughing as hard as her dad, has crawled up his back and is cascading headfirst over his right shoulder into his lap. He controls her descent with one arm. Ruth's youngest son, Adam (eight, also laughing), has crawled up Henry's back and is tumbling over his left shoulder, scrawny bare legs sliding down Henry's chest, head dangling between Henry's firmly planted legs. Henry's other arm is easing Adam down. Mike (three and eager for his turn) stands close to his dad, so close that if he were any closer, he'd be on the other side of him. Henry looks like he's granite; Adam, Laurie, and Mike are gnats.

Forty years after the photo is taken, Adam will post it on Facebook with this caption: *Mt. Hank.*

18

Ramifications are dawning on Henry. The future has been brought into focus. He's lying there, looking like a dazed person, but he starts naming what he sees:

"I'll be wheelchair-bound."

Then:

"I'll have to have a colostomy."

Then:

"There'll be complications."

Then:

"Who knows what's ahead."

Then:

"This is just the beginning."

Later, when we're alone, he whispers, "What's going to happen with us and sex?"

19

For years, I've told Henry what I want him to do and what I don't want him to do if I die first.

"I just know you're going to fall for the first casserole that walks through the door." That's me, warning him to be discriminating. "Remember, if you marry someone who's not cute, it'll be a bad reflection on me. People will assume your first wife wasn't cute, either."

It all started the New Year's Eve we'd been invited to a party at Henry's friend's house, and a woman named Susan was there. We'd been married maybe seven years and were in our thirties. Susan had been divorced for several months. We'd known her when she was married, and she'd always been overweight. Now she was bone-thin. But she'd kept her big bosoms.

In the car on the way home, I asked Henry, "So what did you think of Susan?"

"She was all right." Suddenly, he was concentrating so intently on his driving you'd think it was his first time out.

"No, what did you really think? Like if I were

dead and you were a widower, would you be interested in her?"

"I don't know. Maybe." He put on his clicker to turn. He *never* puts on his clicker when he turns.

"See? That's what I'm talking about. She's the type of woman who's thin for a minute. Sure, she has big boobs, but right after you marry her, her whole body will balloon right back up. You've got to be careful. You should think about marrying Mary or Judy or Debbie." Two close friends and my first cousin. All adorable. But all already married. Did I think they would divorce their husbands the minute I died and Henry was free?

And would his choice of a second wife really reflect on me? Or was it the cruel and outrageous things I was saying about perfectly fine Susan that reflected on me?

No instructions from Henry regarding what I should do if he dies first.

20

"You won the lottery in reverse." That's a surgeon talking. He's not being sarcastic or unkind. He's explaining to Henry the rarity of what happened two days ago.

When he showed up in our hospital room, I thought, *Oh, good! He's going to take over the case.* That would make sense. We have a long history with him. He operated on Henry for spinal stenosis years ago. This surgeon is very approachable. An easy conversationalist. Not what you'd expect. Most surgeons are reserved, uncommunicative—*I* think because they're used to dealing with patients who are sleeping. This surgeon is different.

He pulls a chair closer to Henry and sits down, crossing one leg over the other. He does not break eye contact with Henry. I half sit, half lean on the foot of the bed, eager to hear what the plan is, how we're going to fix this. He's telling Henry that it's a "venous event," not an arterial one. I don't understand this last statement, but I do understand the next thing he says.

He smiles his very genuine smile and states

firmly—without any ambivalence—that Henry will be completely normal in a matter of weeks. Which is the same thing the physiatrist told us right after the epidural. But then the physiatrist gave us the *lasting paraplegia* handout. I don't know what to believe.

Henry and I don't ask any questions. Maybe we're afraid of annoying him by appearing to blame, or even just question, another doctor as to what he might, or might not, have done. The surgeon is saying it's not a lasting problem. If we act as though we fear that it is, he could see us as alarmists, or hysterics. We want him to think well of us. While I'm weighing the pros and cons of trying to find out more, I'm scanning his face to see what he might be holding inside himself.

Still, it's a jolly visit, loose and comfortable. He asks Henry how he's feeling, how they're treating him in the hospital. He listens attentively to the answers. Henry goes into great detail. The surgeon acts as though he has the whole day to sit and chat. We think so highly of him, I decide to put all my trust in what he's saying. Henry will be okay. We just have to be patient.

After maybe thirty minutes, he stands to leave. He takes a step closer to Henry, puts a hand on his arm, then clasps Henry's hand with both of his hands. He holds Henry's hand a little longer than you would for an ordinary, everyday handshake.

"You'll be transferred to a rehabilitation facility next week," he says, letting go of Henry's hand and walking backward in the direction of the door. "I won't be seeing you again." Smile. "Those rehab doctors don't like us poking around."

I don't understand that this means we're pretty much on our own now, that caring for Henry will soon be my full-time job.

21

Surely, now that the weekend is over, we'll boulder in and see things start happening. The epidural took place three days ago, and we're still in the hospital. I want plans. I want action. I want a lot of people looking after my husband. Well, I want *somebody* looking after my husband. I want a move to the rehab facility, where they'll tell us they've seen this sort of thing before and they know exactly what to do to bring on the return to normalcy we've been promised.

·

A trim young woman comes to the room. She gives us her best smile, says she's a physical therapist from the rehab facility, introduces her assistant, a towering guy, hulky, like a bouncer in a bar. His neck is bigger than her waist. She explains they're here to "ambulate" Henry, which means they'll help him walk from his bed to the door, a distance of approximately ten feet. *Good,* I'm thinking. *We're on our way.*

She fastens a thick canvas belt around Henry's waist and grabs it in the back. Henry jokes about the belt, how it makes him look so stylish. Everybody laughs. The assistant, close beside Henry, holds him under both arms. The guy jokes back, "Yeah, man! You're way cool!" We all act as though we're in the middle of something hilarious. The therapist and assistant are keeping him upright and actually sliding his legs forward with their legs. I'm following along behind. If you cut them out of the picture but still let them do their work and all you could see was Henry, you'd be fooled into thinking he's actually walking. But they're the ignition, the motor, and the fuel. He's only a shell.

"I have to stop," Henry suddenly says, and then he seems to just curl into himself, crumpling in their arms. "I'm exhausted." I can't see his face from where I'm standing.

"Quick! Mrs. Goldman! Grab the chair!" the therapist calls over her shoulder. For a second, I'm immobilized. Struck with how far Henry has to go to be "normal." My mouth opens and closes. No sound comes out. It doesn't matter; she's not asking for words. She just wants me to pull the chair over. Which I do. "Now slide it under your husband. There. Okay. Sit here, Dr. Goldman."

The hardy assistant pushes the chair, with Henry collapsed in it, back to the bed. I follow, walking my slowed-down walk, as though the floor is uneven.

I tell myself, *Well, it's a start. A little rough. But still, a start.*

The nurse with the pretty teeth, who told us right after the epidural that she used to work in anesthesiology and was sure Henry would be fine, calls the house today and leaves a message, asking how he is, telling us she's been thinking about him since Friday. I hadn't realized how much I wanted someone connected to the injection to follow up and express concern.

·

Next morning—four days after the epidural—a different physical therapist from the rehab facility comes to Henry's hospital room. A very straight-backed young man. He's able to hold on to Henry's waist (no belt this time) *and* walk him—Henry using a walker—out into the hall. Henry is still profoundly weak and unsteady, but the way he holds his body is brave, purposeful. He's not crumpling. He's sliding his feet along, not exactly a normal stride, more a pushing forward, inch by inch. I follow behind, just in case I need to grab a chair, or my husband—my concentration intense, eyes on him, eyes on the young man, eyes moving rapidly ahead of them, checking to see if anything blocks their way.

The "walk" takes many long minutes. Henry is able to get almost to the nurses' station. Splashy cheers from the nurses behind the desk, as though we're approaching the twenty-six-mile marker of a marathon. Henry waves one arm triumphantly, wobbles, looks as if he could go down, quickly grabs hold of the walker again, rights himself.

The nurses' voices carry us back to the room.

After he's in bed, under the covers, and the therapist leaves, Henry looks up at me. His face is hollow with exhaustion. He's about to speak.

I wait.

After several seconds, he says, between ruptured breaths, "That walk was the hardest thing I've ever had to do."

.

This afternoon, still day four, a third physical therapist from the rehab facility comes. She's young, like the others. She has great posture. But then they all have great posture. I ask if she's here to walk Henry, like the other therapists.

"Absolutely not," she says, raising her nose and taking in the full length of me. The expression that passes over her face—of astonishment, of irritation— seems to have a life of its own. "It would be dangerous and potentially harmful for anyone to walk him without a leg brace to hold his foot in the proper position." She's admonishing me for allowing her colleagues to do such a foolish thing!

22

That cloud of a frown still stirring in her face, the physical therapist is now leaning over Henry, examining him, manipulating one leg, up, down, bending at the knee, up, down, then the other leg, bending that knee, checking his feet and toes, pushing against the sole of each foot, asking him to push back, pressing down on the top of each foot, telling him to raise it against her pressure. I'm afraid to ask any more questions. Instead, I try to read her face. Look for signs. Just a twitch of her eyebrow might be information. But she doesn't give even a hint of what she's finding. Instead, at the end of her exam, she asks him if he'd like to sit in a chair. An enthusiastic yes! She helps him into the vinyl lounge chair beside the bed, tucks pillows around him, covers his legs with a blanket, says she'll check in with us later, and leaves.

This is the first Henry has sat in a chair for any length of time. A smile takes shape at the corner of his mouth. A familiar, easy smile that just gets bigger and bigger. He clicks the remote until he finds a game to watch. *I'm* watching *him*, happy for this so-ordinary sight. Happy, even, to have a husband who loves sports. He could be in the den at home, cheering some team on. "Brilliant play! Brilliant play!" he'd yell at the TV. Or he might question what he considers a ridiculous call, accusing the play-by-play announcer of being the worst he's ever heard, and why did he ever think he should go into sportscasting? I'd be starting dinner in the kitchen, drifting into the den every now and then to see what all the fuss is about. "Watch this replay, Judy!" he'd say, and I'd watch for a minute, then back in the kitchen. Later I'd call out, "Henry!"—to let him know dinner's ready and he can fill the water glasses and set the table.

After the game, a male nurse, who looks like he could be John Goodman's younger brother, helps me put Henry back to bed.

"Would you check my right foot?" Henry asks him. "It feels cold."

The nurse reaches under the blanket. It *is* cold, he reports. He leaves, then brings an extra blanket.

After a while, he returns to check Henry's foot again. Icy cold now.

"Uh-oh," he says to me. "Your husband might have a blood clot." He leaves, comes back with another nurse, talks to me again, not to Henry. Why doesn't Henry speak up? Remind them he's the patient?

"She has more experience than I do." Our male nurse cocks his head in the other nurse's direction. "I want her to check your husband's foot."

"Dr. Goldman, does your foot hurt?" the experienced nurse asks. She speaks directly to Henry. But she talks loudly, as if he's deaf.

"I don't know," he answers. "I don't have any feeling there."

She turns to the male nurse. Yes. A doctor should be called.

·

Later, our same male nurse returns to let us know the doctor on call ordered an ultrasound.

Three and a half hours pass. Henry dozes, wakes, murmurs *What's going on?*, I answer *We're waiting*, he dozes.

When I buzz the nurses' station to ask why the holdup, I'm told there is no one in Ultrasound, and anyway, there are no transporters available. The problem, I'm told, is that the word *stat* was not written on the order. It isn't being treated as a high-priority procedure.

I make a mental note to mention my new word, *stat*, whenever an ultrasound or MRI is ordered. Each new piece of knowledge I want to cup in my hands.

·

Later in the evening, a transporter arrives to take Henry down to Ultrasound. I follow, past a pool of darkness framed by the window. How did it get so late?

We pass Henry's nurse, pushing a medicine cart on the other end of our floor, near the elevator. He tells us we'll be told the results immediately by someone in Ultrasound.

While Henry has the ultrasound, I read *Field & Stream*, the only magazine in this deserted waiting room. Suddenly I hear someone call out, "Judy!" I look up to see the neurologist whom Henry has seen over the years for cluster headaches and back problems. Jim is one of the kindest, gentlest, most concerned doctors we've ever known. A Marcus Welby. With his well-groomed gray hair, rimless glasses, and gracious manner, he could easily leave the medical profession for a successful career playing a minister in the movies.

"I heard what happened to Henry," he says. I look at my watch. Nine o'clock. "I stayed late in the office to finish some paperwork and came right over to see if I can help."

I don't focus on the fact that news of what happened to my husband has already traveled through the medical community. First the surgeon, now the neurologist. I'm too overwhelmed at Jim's coming here, so late in the evening, not even involved in the case, finding me in the depths of the hospital.

In a flurry of words, I tell him everything that has happened. He listens. I talk. He listens. The ultrasound technician interrupts to say the transporter is now taking Henry back to his room. She has an accent I can't place. I ask if they found any blood clots in my husband's leg. She replies that she's not allowed to give out any information.

When she leaves, Jim says, in that quiet, sure

way of his, "The nurse on your floor will give you the results."

I can't thank him enough—just his presence was a moment of light in this dark place. We say good night.

The doors of the elevator open to Henry's floor, and I spot our same male nurse in the hall. I ask him if he has any news about my husband. He says he's not allowed to give us the results. They should have been reported to us in Ultrasound.

·

Hours later, toward midnight, a different nurse comes into the room to deliver the news: no blood clots. Of course, my heart gives a leap. Happy for the results. But I'm learning that everything could change in an instant.

23

Henry's arms:

1. Shirt sleeves rolled up to just below the elbow, sleeves always rolled up.
2. That golden fleece, almost iridescent.
3. Fresh, clean smell (his arms so hairy, they hold the Irish Spring scent for hours after a shower).
4. The architecture of muscle.
5. Thick vines of vein.
6. Reliable. You can count on those arms.

24

Five days since the epidural. This morning, a physician assistant, sent over from the rehab facility, a young man with dark-rimmed glasses, serious and studious in appearance like a librarian, comes to the hospital to do an evaluation in preparation for Henry's transfer. But because a transporter arrives sooner than the PA expects, he isn't able to complete the evaluation.

"No problem," he says, turning to me, then packing up his clipboard, papers, and pen. "I'll finish when your husband gets there."

Another person talking *about* Henry, rather than *to* him. Of course, Henry encourages this kind of response because, much of the time, he's quiet, vaguely inattentive, lost in thought. Or maybe he's just overwhelmed, closed with fear. I can't think of a nice way to say to the various hospital people, *The needle jammed into his back, not his brain. He's still a smart man.*

.

It's nine in the morning. Henry is taken by EMS to a rehab facility, where he's placed in a small double room with a roommate, an elderly, washed-out-looking man. The man's wife, also elderly, also washed out, dead-white hair, dead-white skin, half crouches in a chair pulled close to his bed. They're both so small, so quiet, we can almost pretend they're not here.

The room is very hot. I check the thermostat. Eighty degrees! I'm about to lower the temperature when the wife, in a tiny voice, says, "Please don't do that, honey. The vent is over my husband's bed. He'll get cold."

There's no grab bar above Henry's bed, so he isn't able to roll over or change his position in any way. This is really upsetting for him. Even with his one-thousand-pound legs holding him down, a grab bar enabled him to shift any way he wanted to. He felt strong and capable. He was himself, just with an injury. Now he's handicapped. It's embarrassing for him to ask me to help him roll over. I make a note on my pad to ask an aide or nurse for a grab bar.

But no aide or nurse comes.

Ten o'clock. Eleven. We've now been in this rehab facility for two hours. Henry is wet with perspiration; drops pool off his nose like tears.

"I'm feeling claustrophobic," he says, trying repeatedly to throw himself over to his side but ending up moving maybe an inch. He started out on his back—and is still on his back. The bottom sheet is pulled away from the plastic-covered mattress, because of all that twisting. "It's just so cramped in here, and hot."

Along with the thermostat, the TV is cranked up high. Some game show. The sound is like a hammer driving home a nail. I wipe Henry's forehead with a cold washcloth. He looks as if all the juice has been drained out of him. I'm sure I look the same way. It occurs to me we're turning into that washed-out couple on the other side of the curtain. Maybe if you stay in this room long enough, that's what happens.

25

I've always been fascinated by the way older couples, altered by time, stay rooted, stay married. My parents held hands for almost fifty years. Among family and friends, their marriage was legendary. Even when Mother had Alzheimer's and could no longer recognize anyone, could not utter a word, my father, who was dying of colon cancer metastasized to his lung, bones, and brain, sat by her bed in the nursing home all day, every day, rubbing her legs with Yardley lavender-scented lotion, reading aloud to her, those layered southern vowels of his.

I never miss the section in the Sunday paper that posts the fiftieth-anniversary photos of couples, alongside their wedding photos. I scrutinize their young faces, their old faces, their hair, their clothes. For years, the grooms wore military uniforms; I couldn't wait to get past the World War II weddings, so that I could read personality, character, and temperament into what they were wearing. All that raw material in the wedding couple. The shaping and evolution that would take place over the next fifty years. I want to know their pet names for each other. Their in-jokes. I wonder how many times they hurt each other. How many times they did not call it quits. Two people living through history, becoming doughy caricatures of their younger selves. I love the way they appear so committed to the long term. So willing to make the situation they're in as good as it can be. They're obviously people who don't give up easily.

Back in 1967, when I asked Henry, "Can you picture us growing old together?," I was not only in love with him, I was in love with the idea of a husband and wife moving through life together, youth falling away, both growing slightly stooped, hard of hearing, Henry carrying my purse for me the way old men do, our soft, imperfect last years together.

I didn't expect things to change so swiftly, no warning, us in our sixties.

26

We're by ourselves, on our own, all day. Doesn't any-body work here? Shouldn't someone check in with us? What about the evaluation that was supposed to take place?

Late afternoon, the physician assistant knocks on our door. But he's not here to see how we're doing. Or to complete the evaluation. He's here for one pur-pose: to tell us he'll be switching Henry from a Foley (indwelling) catheter to intermittent catheterization (disposable catheters), to encourage him to urinate on his own.

"We can't leave your husband's catheter in," he says, turning to me. "Too great a risk for infection."

I ask, in my pleasing, steady, keeping-it-together voice (trying hard to get the tone right), if it would be possible to wait until tomorrow morning to remove the Foley catheter. John, our neighbor at home and a urologist, cautioned me that when they remove Hen-ry's Foley, they should not do it late in the day, since no one usually checks to see if a patient urinates during the night. John recommends removing a catheter in the morning when the patient is awake and can try to pee. If it turns out he's unable to pee, he should self-cath around noon, no later than two in the afternoon. And he should be scanned to make sure his bladder has emptied.

The PA says okay, he'll write orders to this effect. I thank him. *That was easy.*

·

At seven in the evening, a nurse comes to check Henry's vital signs. She says she wants to "welcome" and "orient" us to rehab. Ten hours after we arrive! She explains the reason we've been on our own all day is that the rehab doctor assigned to Henry is on vacation this week and the aide assigned to this room didn't report to work today.

She says she's ready to remove his catheter.

I ask if we can possibly wait until morning— again, my pleasing, steady voice—when he'll be awake afterward and can try to urinate.

She says she can't wait; there are orders.

I have to look at *something.* I'm too irritated to look at her. I glance around the room. The walls. The TV hanging high on the wall, bellowing. My chair. Bedside table. Trash can. Everything seems to be leaning. If not leaning, then simmering.

I find her face and explain that the PA told us he'd leave orders for it to be removed tomorrow morning.

No, she says, he did not. The orders say to remove it now. If we wait, my husband could get a urinary tract infection. Which could lead to urosepsis. Which could lead to septic shock. We can't leave a catheter in indefinitely.

I know she's right about the risks. But in weighing risk vs. benefit, in *this* situation, I feel we should leave the catheter in. Not indefinitely. Just until morning.

She and I stare at each other for a second, then look away at the same time.

I search the floor for something—a tissue I attempted to throw in the trash but missed. The paper off one of those flexible straws.

"Well," I say, my voice *not* pleasing, *not* steady, "we want to wait." No more casting my bread upon the waters. No more sweet and polite. The world has turned out to be a stubbornly unsafe place, and sweet and polite don't work.

She says she will bring someone else in to help me understand why this needs to be done immediately.

Minutes later, there are two nurses talking to me about doctor's orders and infection.

I'm not budging.

They both walk past me out the door. Then a supervisor marches in. My first instinct is to say, "Wow! Amazing how many people are available to weigh in now but were unavailable before." But I go with my second instinct: Take a breath.

The supervisor and I stand shoulder to shoulder. She has short hair like mine. She's about my age. We both color our hair. Brown. She repeats what the others have said. I decide to go with a mantra: "We want to wait until morning." She says no, we need to do it now, blah, blah, blah. I repeat, "We want to wait until morning." She shoots me a puzzled look after our second go-round.

What's puzzling is that Henry is not saying a word. I should be used to his uninvolvement. But I'm not. I look over at him. He's awake. But he's not even waving his hand to say *Forget it, Judy.*

She finally says, "Okay. I'll check with the PA. If he says all right, we'll wait till morning. But if he doesn't agree . . ."

"Thank you," I reply. "I really appreciate it." Back to sweet and polite.

She leaves.

Henry smiles up at me. His smile is so wide his teeth show. "You've taken on a whole new persona," he says quietly. He's right. And I feel relief that he has this degree of awareness. He sees that my conciliatory, harmony-seeking, Libra, southern, sweet self has turned into—well, something else. "Yep," he says. "Your hospital personality."

This is the moment we officially switch roles.

I take over.

He gives in.

27

Six memories of Henry and our children:

1. When I was in labor giving birth to Laurie (she was Oxford posterior, faceup instead of facedown), all the pain was in my back. Henry and I had attended Lamaze classes; however, the huff-puff breathing we'd been taught was not working. The only relief came from Henry massaging my back. But he was not just massaging. Hour after hour (it would be thirty-three hours), he put all his strength, his full force, into kneading my lower back. Outside the semicircle of our refuge, nothing existed. "Harder," I pleaded. He rubbed so hard, the following day I had bruises. In the middle of all this, a hospital worker stuck his head into the labor room and asked, in a booming voice, if that was our Volkswagen Beetle parked outside the emergency room.

"Yes," Henry replied, "but I can't leave."

"If you don't move it," the guy said, again at the top of his voice, "you're gonna get towed."

"Go," I said. "I'll be okay."

Henry found the most massive nurse on the floor and asked if she would massage my back as hard as she could while he ran to move his car. And she did. "Harder, harder," I begged. She was powerful, and she was giving it her all. But after Henry returned and we thanked her and she left, I whispered, "Thank goodness you're back. I could not feel her touch at all."

2. With both children, Henry got up for middle-of-the-night feedings. Even early-morning diaper changes. If it was a bad one, Henry would hear me gagging and appear at the changing table. "I've got this," he'd say.

    Very different from other dads in our generation. Whenever we spent a weekend at the beach with another family, the other mom, Henry, and I would be taking care of the kids—cooking mac and cheese, running baths, snapping pajamas, reading bedtime books. The other dad would lounge in front of the TV.

3. In July 1969, when Laurie was three months old, we drove to Miami Beach to visit Henry's parents. On our way back, we stopped for the night at a motel beside the highway, instead of driving straight through, as planned. Henry wanted Laurie to witness the historic moon landing. He woke our baby girl, held her up in front of the TV screen, her face crimped in sleep, little chicken legs dangling, and he said, "See? For the rest of your life,

you can say you saw Neil Armstrong walk on the moon."

4. My biggest peeve with Henry when our children were young was that he would get them all juiced up right at bedtime. Here was their game: Laurie or Mike would flop down flat on the bed, facing the ceiling. Henry stood beside the bed, leaning over, his hands stretched straight out in front, thumbs locked, about to fall forward. "Don't move!" he'd tease. They'd snort with laughter. "Don't close your eyes! No blinking!" Then he'd let himself go, the whole bulk of him, threatening to crush the poor kid. At the very last second, he spread his hands apart to hit the mattress hard on either side of that little head. Henry's face and our child's face would be inches from each other. They'd be fused by laughter. Which led to wilder and wilder jumping on the bed, whacking each other in the head with pillows, diving under the covers all the way down to the foot of the bed.

5. Henry taught Laurie to "throw a ball like a boy," so she'd have a strong tennis serve. He taught Mike how to field—"Lay the glove in the dirt." He coached Mike's T-ball team, Laurie's basketball team. He scheduled himself out of the office for T-ball, basketball, soccer, softball, and baseball games, swim meets and tennis matches. Also, school plays, speech contests, spelling bees, science fairs. He took Laurie's temple youth group

skiing in the mountains. He played basketball in the driveway with Mike and his friends.

When Henry was growing up, his father was in the restaurant business in Miami Beach and worked long hours. He was a loving father but never home. Long after Henry went to bed, his father would wake him up to kiss him good night. Even though his father was an avid sports fan (and an even stronger athlete than Henry), he was never able to go to any of Henry's games. Henry wanted to be steady like his dad—and present.

6. The summer before Mike's sophomore year in high school, we signed him up for two weeks at Duke University's Young Writers' Camp. This would be a big adventure for Mike, a kid who'd been content to spend summers at home, hanging out with friends, shooting baskets in the driveway, playing tennis and golf. He'd gone to camp before—basketball, golf, tennis, or soccer camp. And always with a buddy. Sports were not his only interest, though. He also was a good writer and hoped to become a sportswriter. This writers' camp seemed perfect.

Last day of Writers' Camp, we arrived to pick him up. He spotted us pulling in to the parking lot and ran out of the dorm to greet us.

As soon as Henry and I stepped from the car and the sun was shining down on our son, I saw the earring. It was one of those blue, fake-diamond studs. Just one. Glinting in that one earlobe. Mike! Pierced his ear! Who would ever imagine strait-laced Mike doing such a thing? I wondered what Henry was thinking. I was thinking: *Don't call attention to it, Judy. Be cool. Allow Mike to play loose—without commentary from his mother.*

We stood there, on the concrete, chatting, Mike naming everyone he wanted us to meet—his girlfriend from the Philippines, his roommate from New York City, his hippie, offbeat poetry instructor.

We met them all at the final event, when the campers presented what they'd been writing all week. Then we dropped Mike off at his dorm, waited in the car while he got his stuff. I looked at Henry and tried to read his face. All it was was the face of a father delighted to be with his son again.

"Well, what did you think?" I asked.

"About what?" he said.

"The earring," I said.

"What earring?"

I probably chewed my bottom lip. How could he not notice that his son had pierced his ear?

How could two people—married for so many years, all that cohabitation, parents together—be so different?

The borders between men and women and our wildly differing sensibilities are solidly marked. Women, of course, are noticers. Men are not. Along with a million other absolutes. No one crosses to the other side. The border guards for-ever keep watch.

Unless some major unexpected something causes us to try on a different trait, reposition ourselves. Then we begin sidling over.

28

The catheter is removed this morning, but Henry is unable to pee. Early afternoon, an aide does the first in/out catherization. This will continue every four hours, day and night, until Henry is able to go on his own. If he ever does.

"Good thing they didn't remove the catheter late yesterday," Henry tells me. "No one checked on me the entire night."

The physiatrist who administered the epidural ten days ago is back from vacation and comes for a quick visit with Henry early this morning, before I arrive.

Henry tells him that, as a doctor himself, he would like to be in on any discussions he and his colleagues have about his case.

The physiatrist answers, "Oh, of course you will!"

Henry also asks him to please contact neurological centers around the country to ask if they've had experience with this type of injury and if they know of any treatments or procedures that might speed his recovery.

The doctor says something like "That's a great idea! I'll get on it this week!"

It will be almost six months before we hear from him again.

When Laurie was fifteen, she announced over chicken, rice, and salad at the kitchen table that her French teacher had suggested she attend School Year Abroad, a program for high school juniors and seniors. She'd live with a French family and attend the SYA school, where all the classes would be taught in French, except for math and English.

Mike, twelve, immediately chimed in: "Cool!" He had a mound of chicken bones on the side of his plate. Rice and salad untouched.

"I thought spending your junior year abroad meant junior in college, not high school." Henry.

Laurie picked up her glass of milk, did not take a sip, put it back down.

"Wait, wait," I said, shaking my head yes in Laurie's direction, meaning that she should say more.

She would really like to do it, she said; she loved French, she thought the experience would be good for her, she'd live in Rennes, beginning this coming August, through next June.

"No way will I allow my fifteen-year-old to be

gone an entire school year." Henry emptied his glass of water in a gulp.

"Let's hear her out." I tried a smile.

"Yeah," Mike said, pushing the rice around his plate with the side of his fork. "Let's hear her out." It wasn't unusual for Laurie and Mike to team up. I didn't discover until they were grown that, after Henry and I left the table, Mike always drank Laurie's milk for her and Laurie ate his vegetables.

Laurie answered something like: "It's a really good program, sponsored by Andover and Exeter. Charlotte Country Day is one of a few schools in the country that participate. I'll be home my senior year." She radiated life. "And, Dad, I'll be sixteen when I go. Not fifteen."

"No way." Henry. Grimace. Like he'd already vetoed this idea a thousand times before.

"Here," she said, getting up from the table, grabbing her backpack from the closet in the back hall, where she and Mike kept their school stuff, cleats, bats, gloves, balls, rackets. "Mrs. Beatty said to give you this." She unzipped a pocket, pulled out a brochure, handed it to me. "And you can call her to find out more. And *she* thinks I'll do great there."

"Okay," I said to the brochure, although I'm sure Laurie, Mike, *and* Henry heard that as an okay to School Year Abroad.

Later that evening, after Laurie and Mike had gone to bed, after we'd turned off the news, Henry and I were alone in the den. I told him that if we keep putting up roadblocks we're essentially selling her on the idea. "Let's just see it through," I said. "She won't end up going. I'd bet any amount of money she'll be right here in the fall."

"I'm not sending a sixteen-year-old child to France for a year," he said, pulling himself straighter, eyeing me with something close to distrust. "Period."

I headed into the bedroom. I heard him clicking the TV on again, shuttling through channels, looking for one he liked.

.

Information packets arrived. Laurie and I filled out forms. I ordered her passport. We heard from the host family in Rennes (father in advertising; stay-at-home mom; one son, three years younger than Laurie, Mike's age; two younger daughters). We shopped for clothes and other items, checked off a long list. Farewell party, BON VOYAGE sign the full width of our front yard, gag gifts from her friends. Suitcase bought, ready to pack.

Last-minute, all-caps warning from School Year Abroad: HIGH-LEVEL THREAT OF TERRORISM ... AMERICANS TARGETED ... STUDENTS SHOULD NOT DO ANYTHING WHILE IN FRANCE TO DRAW ATTENTION TO THE FACT THAT THEY'RE AMERICANS ... THEY SHOULD NOT DRESS LIKE TYPICAL AMERICANS OR SPEAK ENGLISH IN PUBLIC PLACES ...

Through it all, Henry remained adamantly

opposed. At night, in bed, his back to me: "What about those anti-American sentiments in France? That really concerns me. And she's at such an impressionable age. She'll be gone so long. How do we know what these French parents are like?"

My answer, one arm easing around his shoulder: "School Year Abroad wouldn't let these kids go to France if they didn't think it was safe. And don't we believe that our children know what's best for themselves? Laurie is so sure this is right for her."

I had changed from believing she wouldn't end up going to believing going would be a good thing. Henry, obviously, had not changed at all. How I pushed this dramatic decision through, I don't know. I wonder if I was at all surprised to steamroll such an important move for our daughter right over Henry's back.

.

On an early-August day cooled by a New England breeze, our family arrived at Logan Airport in Boston to see Laurie off for her junior year abroad. In a private room, away from the gritty noise of the main terminal, we made a wide circle with the other families. The School Year Abroad administrator, a lanky, Ichabod Crane, New England prep school kind of guy, addressed the sixty students—thirty juniors, thirty seniors—seated cross-legged on the floor, inside the tight arrangement of folding chairs we parents and sisters and brothers filled. Laurie looked *so young*— her mouth open, eyes wide as full moons.

Because security was pretty nonexistent in 1985, you could accompany passengers to the gate. The four of us stood beside the open door leading to the tarmac, Mike and Laurie saying jokey sibling things that weren't really jokes about how they were going to miss each other. Then hugs and kisses all around. Then Laurie joined her new classmates up the steep steps into the plane.

Henry, Mike, and I waved big waves that Laurie, now peering at us through a foggy little window, could not miss.

Suddenly, I realized I was still holding her winter coat over my arm. I'd held on to it for so long it had become a part of me.

I dashed out the airport door, into the cool, up the stairs, into the plane, Laurie came forward, I handed off the coat, she headed back down the long aisle to her seat, I turned and left.

When the fresh air hit my bare arms, they suddenly felt *so* cold.

Back into the airport. Henry, Mike, and I stood at the large plate-glass window, watching the plane taxi down the runway, lift, veer off. We stood there and watched, until the plane vanished, swallowed by air. At that moment, I felt something like a fist to my stomach. A tiny fit exploding inside me. I turned to Henry. "I think we just made the biggest mistake of our lives."

He wrapped his arms around me, pulled me so close my face got buried in his chest, all wool and warmth. "It's going to be fine," he said. "In fact, I was just thinking she's doing exactly what she should be doing."

.

This was not the first time he and I had been in different worlds, then switched. Like two sides of a dime.

I'm the real worrier. Always have been. When Laurie would hang batlike from the highest monkey bars in the park, I was already envisioning her in the back of an ambulance, arms and legs crushed to powder. When Mike headed out the door to bike to a neighborhood friend's house, overwrought words traveled from my mouth: "Be careful! Look out for cars! Watch for loose gravel in the street! Keep your wits about you!"

But during their teenage years, Henry was the one who waited up until they came in at night. I slept blissfully. I slept blissfully *because* he was waiting up.

If he worried about our daughter going to France for a year, I had the luxury of not worrying. He'd take care of that for both of us. As though it was useless energy for two people to worry at the same time. One of us would take the hit and allow the other to relax. When it got too burdensome, the other would take over. Swapping our roles back and forth, that little track of accommodation, is never something we expect to do. But when it happens, it feels familiar, almost inevitable.

31

The Physical Therapy Department in the rehab facility is a large, overlit, carpeted room, wide open like a warehouse. Athletic and attractive physical therapists, with their straight backs, work with patients in every stage of disability, many of them quadriplegics, some teenagers, all trying their hardest to come back. Such earnest expressions—as they grip the parallel bars, lift weights, pull themselves up and down the little wooden staircase block in the middle of the room. They teach Henry and me that, even though he travels to physical therapy in a wheelchair and he's dying to ditch that wheelchair, we should count our blessings.

"I have nothing to complain about," Henry whispers to me. "Nothing at all."

"I know," I whisper, "I know."

His prognosis? Maybe he'll be able to recoup some of what he's lost. Maybe he will eventually walk with the aid of a walker. But not a single rehab doctor or physical therapist is making any promises.

Therapy is difficult. Painful. He throws himself into each leg lift, each push and pull, each step he attempts holding on to the parallel bars. I can see his jaw muscles working. I move from station to station with him, as though we're tethered. I count with him when he loses track of the repetitions, cheer him on by telling him he's a John Wayne. I make sure his therapists hear me saying he's a John Wayne, even though they're too young to know who John Wayne is. I tell them they've got the former city racquetball champion here. I wonder if it's obvious how badly I want them to know what my husband was once capable of, how I want them to know I care about him, that he's important to someone.

Important to many, in fact. To Mike, who comes often. To Brooke and bright-eyed, one-year-old Tess, who likes pushing the button that makes Pop's bed go up and down. Laurie, Bob, and their three-year-old identical twins drive in from Durham when they can. Lucy and Zoe, their coppery red hair (like Henry's, before he turned gray), push Pop in his wheelchair, up the hall, down the hall. Friends visit. Henry's sister, Ruth; my brother, Donald (now living in Charlotte); brother-in-law, Chuck (my sister, Brenda, died of cancer two months before Henry's epidural); our nephews and nieces; our cousins.

I wheel Henry out to the back patio and we sit with our company at one of the wobbly umbrella tables. Henry tells me to fold a paper napkin into a tiny square and wedge it under the table leg. Now, that's better. It still feels like I'm playing a role. Hosting a garden party. I try to be the hospitable, lively hostess. Henry plays his part, too. No complaints.

Funny stories about rehab. We shade our eyes against the sun as it rises high in the sky. All around us, aides push patients outside, then back in, aides take breaks, smoke cigarettes, eat their bag lunches.

.

One day the physical therapist wheels Henry and two other patients—a man and a woman, probably in their eighties—around a tall, round table in the middle of the room. He helps each of them to stand. The other patients are white-haired, knobbed, bent over. I hang back. The therapist explains they're going to play a dice-and-chips game, and the goal is to amass the most chips. Of course, we all know the real goal for these people who are relearning how to stand is to be distracted enough by the game that they don't notice how long they're upright. If they start to feel unsteady, they can grab the edge of the table.

Henry enters in as though he's a croupier in Las Vegas. "Okay, roll those dice, sweetheart! They're hot, they're hot!" He's also coaching the others on the fine points of gambling. ("Keep your poker face, buddy . . .") He counts out the chips for each person. Then, with great drama, pinkie raised, he slides the stacks across the table. The others seem a little confused by the game. I'm guessing they're stroke victims. But they laugh heartily with Henry. The woman, whose teeth click a little when she talks, adds her own Vegas banter. "Ohhh, baby!" she croons. For these few minutes, we all forget where we are.

32

Five years before the epidural, back pain was making it harder and harder for Henry to work. In fact, the long hours and awkward posture of standing and bending over patients while examining their eyes exacerbated his pain. Sometimes, between exams, he would have to lie on the floor to get relief. Finally, Laurie, Mike, and I held something like an intervention. The three of us, surrounding their father in our den, using all sorts of combinations of logic, insisted this endurance course was no longer possible. You have to retire, we declared. I'm not ready, he said. But working is harming your health, we insisted. I'm too young to stop, he said. But your back, look what you're doing to yourself, we argued. Finally: Okay, okay. He was sixty-two; I was sixty.

Months later, he and I were reading in bed. I turned off my light, dropped my book and reading glasses on the bedside table, turned toward him, and said, "I think we need a new division of labor."

He let the newspaper drift down to his chest, shifted a little to face me.

"So," I said. "Our situation has changed." I flipped my pillow to the cool underside and sank in. "I'm still working. And you're not. I think we need to look at the jobs to be done around the house. I know two different couples where the husband and wife each do their own laundry. What do you think about that for a start?"

"I don't want to do my own laundry." He swiveled onto his back, searching for a place on the ceiling to rest his eyes. Then he turned completely away from me, weight on one shoulder, arms tightly crossed, newspaper crushed beneath him.

"Why not?" I asked his upper arm.

"I just don't." He pulled out the newspaper, made a big point of rattling the pages, searching for that one article that he would now read instead of continuing with me. Only, he would say one last thing: "Let's not talk about this now."

So I said one last thing: "Fine. But we're going to have to talk about it at some point."

He didn't answer.

I have a theory about marriage and resentment. If it's just one tiny annoying thing your spouse does and you really don't mind all that much, you can just overlook it. But if you feel resentment building, then this is a sign something has not been discussed that needs to be discussed. You're hurting your health *and* the health of the relationship. You'll soon find yourself living with what's left. So I say let resentment be your guide.

I waited a couple days before bringing it up again.

The crux of my argument: I was writing my second novel. I was editing manuscripts for beginning writers, teaching workshops. I was doing the grocery shopping, cooking, cleaning up after dinner, taking care of the laundry, house, yard, errands. Yes, he paid the bills, managed insurance and taxes. But I felt I was doing more than my share.

No luck in even discussing. Defensive wrangling on his part. Long, rolling sighs on my part—and offensive wrangling. But his attitude didn't make sense to me. This was a man who had always done his share of the work. What was going on?

It took a third try—maybe a week later—before we finally began a real conversation about the jobs to be done and how to divide them. It turned out my suggestion that we each do our own laundry had been the sticking point. This felt to him as though I was asking for a divorce. Couples who do their own laundry, he said, are a step away from doing everything separately.

I pictured our conjugal clothes hamper in the linen closet. My panties and his underwear, his socks and my bras. The jumble of all that.

I'd sold him short. This wasn't about labor. It was about love.

Okay. I'll keep doing the laundry, I said.

He immediately volunteered to do the grocery shopping, after-dinner cleanup, make the bed, run errands—drugstore, dry cleaner, shoe repair. He'd continue taking care of our finances. I said I'd make out the grocery list and do the cooking and take care of the yard. (Now I worried, was I doing enough?) He would set up the coffee at night. I'd pour two orange juices in the morning.

33

I do not love those movies that fill you with anxiety because you're waiting for one person to do something awful to another person. Henry, on the other hand, does love them.

When we got married, I thought I'd change. Or, rather, I let him talk me into changing. Which means, in 1971, I reluctantly went with him to see *Straw Dogs*, starring Dustin Hoffman. The plot: A young American and his English wife move to rural England and face increasingly violent local harassment. Mainly, what I remember are the farm implements and the creative ways they were used.

I don't remember much more because I spent most of the movie out in the lobby, alone, in irritable silence, waiting for it to end and for Henry to come out so we could go home. In those days, lobbies were dim and deserted while a movie played. I sat in that worn velvet chair, listening for footsteps, imagining people with bad intentions standing over me, whispering in my ear. I kept jerking around to see if somebody had come up behind me.

When the movie was finally over and Henry joined me, I walked three steps ahead of him all the way to the car, made sure he saw the set of my shoulders, straight and fixed, my purposeful and self-righteous stride.

I don't think we hammered the whole thing out for years. But, eventually, we did reach an understanding.

I did not see *Jaws* in 1975 or *The Deer Hunter* in 1978 or *Platoon* in 1986 or *The Silence of the Lambs* in 1991 or *Pulp Fiction* in 1994 or *Saving Private Ryan* in 1998. Or any of the violent movies that came after. He did, with a friend or son or son-in-law. The bony wrestling that couples engage in.

34

I'm a great advice-giver. In fact, I have an uncanny ability to know what everyone else should be doing with their lives. The main character in my first novel was a therapist on the radio. I gave her that career because I would *love* to be a therapist on the radio. I have theories about everything.

.

My theories on marriage:

1. I believe each person should feel he or she is the lucky one. If only one partner feels that way, the marriage is in trouble before the invitations go out. The one who feels lucky will spend a lifetime trying to convince the other that he, too, ought to feel lucky. *I am a catch! I am desirable!* You can never, ever talk another person into thanking his lucky stars he got you.
2. My first rule about arguing: No matter how mad you get, you are never allowed to say "I'm leaving." Or "I want a divorce." Once you and your spouse

agree to ban those threats, you can go ahead and get as angry as you like, knowing neither of you will take it to the next (and final) step.

Early on, during those moments when the rosy heart of our marriage first threatened to turn dark, it would never have occurred to Henry or me to mention divorce. But then the years flipped by.

"That's it! I'm through!" he yelled in the middle of a hot one, car keys in hand, out the back door.

"I hate living with you!" I blurted out, stomping after him through the den, the kitchen, heading toward the back hall.

By the time I got to the hall, he'd slammed the back door. I opened it, positioned myself on the brick steps, watched him storm out to the driveway, into his car.

"Don't come back!" I yelled. "Just go!"

"That's exactly what I plan to do," he yelled, loud enough for the neighbors to the right of us and behind us to hear.

"Good!" Making sure those same neighbors heard what I had to say, too.

We were saying whatever it took to let the other person know just how mad we were.

Which scared us both to death.

Later that night, I heard him unlock the back door, take the stairs two at a time up to my office. I was jabbing pages with my pen, dashing off angry poems, hoping to die as soon as possible so that he'd find my poems and feel terrible.

He said, quietly, "Do you want to talk?"

"Yes," I answered.

He told his side.

I told mine.

Somehow, we were able to listen.

We made up.

Then we tackled the larger issue. We decided just what would be sayable during an argument and what would be forever off-limits.

Both of us remember that particular fight—although neither of us remembers what it was about. Still, this many years later, we hold tight to the rules we made in the calm, sensible aftermath of all that unhinged anger.

Of course, no one should stay in a marriage just because of a promise never to resort to the D-word. If a marriage is unhappy, divorce is a legitimate option. You have only one life; you shouldn't spend it lurching from one tortured moment to another. But assuming the marriage has solid scaffolding, agreeing to limits on what you can and cannot say will give you more freedom. You can fall all the way backward, knowing there's someone there to catch you.

3. Every husband and wife, at some point in their marriage, probably consider divorce. There's that well-known TV interview with Gwyneth Paltrow's parents, actress Blythe Danner and director-producer Bruce Paltrow. The interviewer asked how they had managed to stay married for such a

long time, living in Hollywood, where divorce is so prevalent. Blythe Danner said something about their ability to communicate, their sensitivity to the other's feelings, their love for each other, honor, respect, devotion, loyalty. Bruce Paltrow said, "We never wanted a divorce at the same time."

4. If we could view our past boyfriends standing in a row (like those police lineups in *The New Yorker* cartoons), we'd see that each represents our reaction to the one who came before. If what we didn't like about boyfriend #1 was his lack of athleticism or his introversion, it's a sure bet boyfriend #2 will be an extroverted jock. By the time we marry, we believe we know what we're looking for. And we usually get it. Probably more than we bargained for. A friend of mine, a powerful and independent woman, wanted a man who was at least as powerful as she. Her husband was so powerful— unbelievably hardheaded—she couldn't live with him. They're now divorced. Another friend, whose father abandoned her family when she was young, wanted someone so loyal he would never stray. She got what she wanted. Her husband is loyal, ever-present, suffocating.

What happens when you get what you want and you actually *love* what you get, but then the very quality you cherish disappears?

Here's the real question: *Does* it disappear? Or do qualities get dismantled and reconstructed? Twist themselves into new permutations?

35

All week Henry's physical therapists have been preparing him to leave on a "pass," to see if he's ready to manage living at home.

Sensation has returned to his left leg and foot, but it's patchy—only in spots. His right leg is still paralyzed. He has what is called a "drop foot," which means he can't raise his right foot toward his shin, can't lower that foot, and can't move his toes. His walk is a slapping motion. He has neuropathy in both feet, worse in the right, so he does not feel the position of his feet. Because he can't sense where his feet actually are, it's hard for him to maintain his balance. That great frame of his, now the frame of a fragile person. Hunched over a walker, he is able to take a couple steps, but mostly he uses a wheelchair.

He's been eagerly anticipating today, so excited about going home, even for just a day. If the visit goes well, there's a good chance he'll be discharged the day after tomorrow.

Mike picks me up and we arrive at the rehab facility around eight in the morning. We're both in such festive moods that when we speak we practically sing. I'm so happy I feel light-headed.

When we get to Henry's room (he was moved into a single room two days ago), we see that no one has turned on the lights, and his wheelchair is drawn close to the window. We walk in and, in spite of the dimness, we see that he's not actually facing the window. He's facing the wall. Not reading, not watching TV. Just sitting there. He doesn't wheel around to greet us.

"Hi, Dad," Mike says, hitting the switch by the door.

Wheelchair still turned to the wall. No answer.

"Henry? Are you okay?" I ask, my voice turning tinny.

Mike and I walk around the bed and each give him a kiss on his forehead at the same time, one of us kissing him over his right eye, the other over his left. That's when we see that flinty look on his face, the one where he presses his lips together. It's a look that says he's mad. Or sad.

Earlier this morning, he says, a nurse told him the doctor had not written orders for a pass, so he can't go home today. Why? Because the family must receive instruction in transferring him from his wheelchair to a car, and that has not taken place. Who does the instructing? A physical therapist. But because it's Sunday and there are so few physical therapists on duty, no one has the time to do it.

"So I'm not going home today." His voice is whisper-thin, almost quivering. He's mad *and* sad.

"And whose fault is it they didn't give us instruction? All this time, they never even mentioned it?"

The point is, for Henry, the thought of going home today was like a bright ship floating on the horizon. Going home represented an achievement. A reward for hard work. Moving on.

I decide to let Mike answer Henry, if there is an answer. I march out to the nurses' station and ask the first nurse I see if I can speak with a doctor, if not in person, then by phone. She tells me our doctor is on vacation. *Again?* Well, I ask, could she have another doctor call me?

"Sure," she says. "But it's Sunday. So it might take some time."

Henry, Mike, and I wait in the room. We're not talking. Not even the tiniest shifting of breath. Henry still faces the wall. Mike and I stand, wedged between Henry's wheelchair and the wall, like two stiff cushions. The silence in the room feels penetrating. It's hard to imagine that Henry, Mike, and I would all be together and not be saying a word.

Finally, the phone in the room rings. I pick up, first ring.

It's a doctor. She says, with the sharp tongue of authority, that there's nothing she can do. It's a rule.

I tell her I'm sure my son and I can get my husband from the wheelchair into our car. My son is really tall and strong. Can't we just bend this rule?

She says if she disregards the rule, they could be held liable. He can't go home today.

She is nothing if not certain. And the rule is sounding more and more rock-hard. I could easily break down in a paroxysm of anger. Anger at her. At our absent rehab doctor. At our absent physiatrist. At all that's absent from our lives. But I'm willing myself to take things one at a time. No exclamation points. I force myself to adjust to the fact that he's not going home today. Which is not a tragedy. It's a disappointment, that's all. And we can deal with it. There are worse things in this world than a delay in going home for a trial visit. And. He *will* go home, for good, on Tuesday.

"How does this affect his discharge on Tuesday?" I ask.

"Oh, it's unlikely he'll be able to go home then," she says.

I shake my head, as though I can shake her words away. But they're there. With a heavy black outline around them. I feel a flush spreading across my skin. I know my face and neck are red. I didn't want to get angry. I wanted to be that wife who rolls with the punches. That wife whom everyone in the rehab facility likes and admires. I look at my watch. Nine-thirty. All this time we're wasting when we could be home!

Okay. New order of business: Someone needs to give us instructions. Anyone. Then we go home. Today. This morning. Now. Then he goes home for good on Tuesday. I will push that into being.

I call the Physical Therapy Department. Surely there is one physical therapist who can give us instructions.

Nobody answers the phone.

Okay. I need a supervisor. Supervisor of nursing. Supervisor of physical therapy. *Any* supervisor. (I'm unstoppable! I could scale towers!)

But. No supervisor.

I try Physical Therapy again. A therapist picks up. A very pleasant voice. She asks questions. I explain. I try to hold down the insistence in my voice. She's being quite sympathetic. My anger is fading, barely there now, like a sore scabbing over. She says she'll be happy to meet us at the main entrance of the hospital to teach us how to transfer Henry from the wheel-chair to our car.

I race out into the hall to tell the nurse. Can hardly get the words out in a logical sequence. Unimpressed, she says she must speak with the physical therapist herself to verify what I'm telling her.

Back to the room. Wait with Mike and Henry. The three of us struggle again with the silence. For all we know, the whole thing could still break down.

After maybe fifteen minutes, the nurse leans through the doorway.

"We have our pass!" she says. *We? All of a sudden she's on our team?* "I'll call for someone to wheel your husband down."

·

Our instruction involves holding Henry while he takes one step from the wheelchair into the car; then we lift his legs around to the front. Why was it so important that we "learn" this? It is nothing compared to what I've had to do these past weeks—alone—without any training, when no nurse or aide was available.

It's after eleven (three hours since we arrived at the rehab facility) when Mike finally pulls away from the curb.

.

After we get Henry and his wheelchair up the back steps, inside the house, into the kitchen, he begins to cry. Mike and I are crying, too. I cross the room to where I keep the Kleenex box. I open the drawer beneath my collection of ceramic pitchers on the counter and pull out one, two, three Kleenex. Sixteen days since Henry and I walked out, double-locked the back door, and drove to the outpatient clinic for the epidural. We were supposed to be back home in an hour and a half. We're home now, in this kitchen—and the kitchen feels so normal. The pine table I found years ago at a flea market in the mountains looks just like we left it sixteen days ago. You can still see the hole burned through the wood from the Hanukkah candle that fell out of the menorah when the children were little. The four chairs that used to belong to Henry's mother, white then, now painted red, and the brass light fixture over the table. Normal. The wide window, quiet backyard, birdfeeder. Normal. The birdfeeder just needs seed.

36

Henry and I always left the light burning over the kitchen table. Then we double-locked the back door and headed down our too-steep driveway for our two-mile evening walk through the neighborhood. All around us, insects buzzed. Sometimes we held hands. Sometimes Henry put his arm about my shoulders and pulled me close, causing me to walk sideways like a crab. That's when he would whisper in my ear, as though intent on a world-class seduction, "Ben and Jerry's?"

I never said no.

I always got one scoop of vanilla in a cup. Henry sampled at least two flavors, usually three. He took his time deciding. "What kind are you having?" he'd ask, as if I ever picked anything other than vanilla. When I pointed this out, he said, "Well, there *was* that one time you got peach." I worried we were holding up the line, but his only worry was which flavor he should try next. "Could I sample Peanut Butter Cup? Okay. Now. Chunky Monkey. And how's that Chocolate Fudge Brownie?" Finally, he'd make up his mind. Each time, something different. Over the years, he tasted every flavor on the board, except the low-fat ones.

We'd take our ice cream outside and sit on the low brick wall under the moonlight, telling each other what we'd done during the day—his workout at the Y, my writing, our children. Everything we'd saved up to tell. Our words like little toasts to a marriage. Innocent promises that life would continue to work out just the way we wanted it.

37

Home. For good. After eighteen days, it feels like we've finally found some lost place.

Henry sits on the sofa, clicking channels, wheelchair close by, while I rush around him, pushing the leather chair, ottoman, Parsons chair, and end table closer in. I lug the coffee table into the laundry room. Not much room with the washer and dryer, but if I fold up the ironing board ...

Now there's a wide, clear path through the den. Henry can wheel easily from the kitchen all the way to our bedroom.

Every four hours, I help him self-cath. We force ourselves to stay up until midnight our first evening, so that we can cath right before turning out the light. This way, we have to get up only once during the night, for the four-o'clock cath.

Now, we're up for the eight a.m. cath. Such a different kind of intimacy with a spouse. It's not about sex. It's about pee. Leaning over him, helping with the tubing, I notice a swelling in his right foot. As soon as we're done, I call the rehab doctor's nurse, leave a message asking what we should do.

At noon, I drive him to the rehab building for his first outpatient physical therapy appointment. We have orders for therapy three times a week, with discharge instructions that the first three weeks of outpatient therapy are crucial for his recovery.

I stop at the curb, pull the wheelchair out of the trunk, roll him into the lobby, leave for the parking garage across the street. When I return, he tells me that while he was waiting for me, his rehab doctor happened to walk by. Henry asked him about his swollen foot. The doctor didn't look at the foot (I guess I can be okay with that—a lobby is not exactly the place for an examination), but he said not to worry, that if the swelling travels up his leg, Henry should notify him. Henry seems reassured. I'm not.

I wonder if I'll ever get to feel lax again. Or is this it? Mighty effort after mighty effort to get to the next step, and the next, and the next.

•

An outpatient physical therapist evaluates Henry, is very rushed, and, instead of an hour evaluation, she can give him only twenty minutes. I sit (balance) on a pile of rubber mats off to the side. I can see that the evaluation is difficult for Henry; she has him do things he has never done. He tries hard to walk with her four-pronged cane, but it's practically impossible.

She holds on to the elastic waist of his sweatpants while he totters in front of me.

At checkout, the receptionist tells me there are no appointments available for the next three weeks. "But his discharge orders say to have physical therapy at least three times a week. And it's important to start now," I say. Henry does not hear any of this; he's in his wheelchair, parked near the door. I feel a dull pressure in my temples.

"I'm sorry," she says, sweeping her hand across her scheduling book, as if to say it's the scheduling book's fault. "There's just nothing here."

A smile is fixed to my face like plastic. I plead. I press. She scrutinizes her book, burrowing her head, glasses down to the end of her nose. Finally, she finds one appointment with an assistant therapist for next week. But there are none this week and none the week after next.

"In May," she says—May is three weeks away!— "your husband can begin seeing a certified physical therapist three times a week."

May is a month I normally think of as being rich with promise. Without raising the blinds, you sense the light is different. That clear degree of change. Everything flowering. Azaleas, dogwoods. Japanese maples brightening. But today, the words *in May* make me cold.

.

The next morning, I spring into action, spend hours on the phone back and forth with a different receptionist at outpatient physical therapy, with a supervisor, with the supervisor's supervisor, trying to get appointments with a certified physical therapist three times a week, beginning immediately. I keep reminding myself: Everything that is solid is not necessarily solid. I can change things.

"We're sorry," the Head of All Supervisors says, "but we have a lot of patients we need to take care of, and we're booked for the next three weeks. Anyway, didn't we find you an appointment for next week?"

"Well, yes. But only one appointment. And with an *assistant* physical therapist."

"Mrs. Goldman, you need to understand that an assistant is just as good as a certified physical therapist. Besides, there'll be a lot of certified physical therapists in the gym working with other patients while your husband is having his therapy, and if the assistant has any questions, she can ask them."

"It sounds like you need more certified physical therapists," I bark. "Do you have plans to hire more?" I'm not only in charge of my husband's recovery, I'm also taking on the labor force at outpatient physical therapy.

"You have to understand, hiring is a process and takes time," Ms. Supervisor says. "We need to take care of the patients who are already coming to us."

My hospital personality takes over, like a current. "That doesn't make any sense," I fire back, with barely a pause. "You need to take care of *all* your patients."

·

Thirty hours after I left a voicemail message, the rehab doctor's nurse returns my call. I tell her about the swollen foot. She says it's nothing to worry about. I tell her about the situation with physical therapy. *That* gets her attention! "It's appalling they can't find time for you. I'll get on it Monday morning." Her exact words.

We won't hear from her again.

·

Here's the heart of it: Over and over, in this world we now find ourselves in, I save Henry from crisis. *Some* crises. At the same time, over and over, *other* crises occur, ones I have no control over.

Which reinforces two conflicting messages, two opposing truths:

Truth #1: I can't protect him. No matter how watchful I am, vigilant and alert to every possible danger, I can't protect him. Even if nothing escapes my attention, even if I check behind every doctor, nurse, and aide, weigh every decision, I can't avert every crisis, swoop in and save my husband.

Truth #2: I can protect him. If I'm watchful and vigilant and alert to every possible danger, if nothing escapes my attention, if I check behind every doctor, nurse, and aide, weigh every decision, I can swoop in and save my husband.

Regardless of the mounting evidence of #1, I seem to be relying on #2.

38

Weeks before Henry had the epidural, Laurie called to ask us to meet her and Bob and their three-year-old twins on a Sunday morning at a Cracker Barrel outside Salisbury. Not a restaurant any of us would normally choose, but it's halfway between their house in Durham and ours in Charlotte.

Our two cars pulled into the parking lot at the exact same moment. Before they even got out, I saw the expectant looks on all their faces, as if the whole lot were filled with friends arriving for a surprise party—which, in a way, our gathering did turn out to be.

A ponytailed hostess seated us; Lucy and Zoe ate the little pats of butter while we waited for our waitress; we ordered grilled cheese sandwiches all around, which my mother used to say was the safest thing on a menu. And then, just before we started to think about dessert, Laurie announced, bright-eyed and bright-voiced, "Big news! We're moving to Charlotte!"

The restaurant was swarming with people—families dressed up from church, toddlers begging for candy they'd seen displayed at toddler eye level in the shop adjacent to the restaurant, old people on their walkers and canes, tired travelers. I suddenly found myself drifting inside and outside the chatter surrounding me, including the talk at our table. *This isn't happening! Laurie's moving back! I can help with the girls! They'll spend the night with us! They'll see their cousin Tess more! I can pop in at their house! They can pop in at ours!* Inebriated thoughts in a too-full head. Everything about to tip me over.

They'd spoken with a realtor in Durham, who strongly urged them to renovate their kitchen. Little by little, over the years, they had updated the rest of their 1920s bungalow but had not tackled the kitchen. "Are you sure you want to get into that now?" I asked. "Why can't you just sell the house as is and save yourselves all that trouble and money?" *Why can't I go five minutes without giving advice?* In the end, we offered to keep Lucy and Zoe for a week so that they could do the renovation.

.

And then, Henry's epidural.

The very next day, which was the beginning of spring break at Lucy and Zoe's pre-school, we were supposed to meet them at a restaurant near Salisbury. Laurie had said she'd find some cute place, other than Cracker Barrel, online. Henry and I would bring Lucy and Zoe back home with us for the week. Bob would take the week off from work and Laurie would take a break from freelancing, and the two of them would redo their kitchen.

Instead of Bob taking the week off from work to get the kitchen done, he took the week off to take care of Lucy and Zoe while Laurie came to Charlotte to help Henry and me sort out our lives. When she returned home, she and Bob—evenings after work, when the girls were in bed—thrust themselves into the renovation. The linoleum floor ended up being impossible to pull up cleanly, the new countertops did not work right, unfinished cabinets needed more work and more paint than they'd bargained for, they removed the old sink, the new sink didn't come in, days without a sink, days of washing dishes in the bathtub. Saturdays, Laurie took the girls to breakfast at Elmo's, then to their little gymnastics class, then to Chick-fil-A for lunch and play on the climbing equipment, then home for a nap, all of which gave Bob extra hours to work on the house.

A perfect symmetry: Chaos wrapped itself around Laurie and Bob, just as—and because—it had wrapped itself around Henry and me.

·

Now Henry has been discharged from the rehab facility. Laurie calls:

"Mom, how 'bout if Lucy, Zoe, and I come for a few days? I'm dying to see Dad at home."

"Well," I say. "I don't know." How do I say what I really want to say? *No, no, don't come! I can barely cope with taking care of one person! I don't want any more people in this house! Especially two three-year-olds!*

"What do you mean you don't know?" Her voice turns leathery.

"Well, I'm not sure I can handle y'all being here. It's really hard taking care of Dad and it's all so new and I just don't know." I tuck the phone into my neck and fold my arms to protect myself—but protect myself from what?

"No, *I'm* coming to help *you*! Not for *you* to help *me*! If I'm there, you won't have to do everything by yourself!"

"Wel-l-l . . ." I say, drawing the word out, hoping I'm giving her time to rethink.

"Mike is there! You're there! I can't *not* be there!" She's hurt. Angry. Extremely angry. "This is ridiculous! I don't care what you say, I'm coming!"

·

And she does come. And it's fine. In fact, more than fine. They spend two nights. She's a huge help to both Henry and me. She cooks. She helps Henry do his exercises. She takes Lucy and Zoe to the park when we need quiet. But, most important, Lucy and Zoe brighten the rooms of our house, as if they're made of light.

I could be my own attorney and Laurie's attorney, both at the same time: Of course, she wanted to be here. She must have been shocked to hear me tell her not to come. When have I ever said anything like that to her, or to Mike? But from my perspective, I couldn't imagine more bodies in my house—especially bodies I normally take care of.

I was being shortsighted.

We all just need to reinvent ourselves. Figure out how to break into the new paradigm.

39

Laurie and the girls leave. We're on our own again.

It's starting to feel like we're always awake. Like when you have a newborn in the house and you're constantly scrutinizing the nursing schedule to try to get a longer stretch of sleep. Self-cathing every four hours is wearing us out.

We decide to experiment. Self-cath every eight hours.

A huge improvement that opens up our days and nights.

But his bladder gets too full. Which is uncomfortable. And not safe.

We scale back to every six hours, which is still better than the four-hour schedule we'd been on.

The swelling in his right foot has moved up his leg. Should we call the doctor?

I put my hand on his forehead: warm. Is he getting an infection from all this self-cathing? I take his temperature. No fever.

I feel cold spots up and down his right leg and in his foot. Should I be concerned?

He is using his walker more, but he's drained at the end of the day. This is a man who never felt fatigue, never took a nap. Never uttered the words "I'm tired."

I see him clenching his whole body just to complete one set of home exercises.

Here's our schedule: I help him cath around six in the morning, strap on his AFO (leg brace), then his sneakers. Breakfast. A rest. Then he walks around the house with his walker. He showers, using a bench, and gets dressed. Lunch. Noon cath. Home exercises. Another rest. Some afternoons, family or friends visit. They tell him, "You're taking this so well." Which helps, I can see. The soup and pies they bring, their attention, are notes of hope for both of us. After they leave, we're buoyed. But we also worry we're over-burdening them, frightening everybody off with our needs. And we're judgmental of the friends and family who don't call or come, who don't bring us food, who fall short in all the ways we dream up. We can't help ourselves. Late afternoon, Henry caths. Walks around the house. Then dinner. TV. Last cath, around midnight. Get ready for bed. Set alarm for six a.m.

Mostly, our day is spent keeping him comfortable and functioning. Which, surprisingly, can have its own sweetness. When concerns are immediate and one's world is confined, the commonplace can feel almost sacred. There are many honeyed moments—dinner at the wicker table on the screened porch, the air turning warm; six-o'clock news in the den, the intersection of our world and the larger world; reading in bed, the two of us connected by the tick of the ceiling fan.

Moments like these remind me of the recurring dream I had as a child: I'd be digging with my bare fingers in the dirt beneath the huge forsythia in the backyard. All of a sudden, I'd unearth handfuls of nickels and dimes, shiny as eyes.

Ninety percent of the time we're optimistic. The bad things that happen end up being not so bad. And, besides, when it comes to health problems, everyone has something. The two of us haven't been singled out for misfortune. And we're certainly not entitled to be in tip-top shape forever. In fact, we're grateful for the progress he's made and hopeful that his nerves will keep repairing.

Ten percent of the time, though, we're self-centeredly despondent about the dramatic turn his life took a month ago, angry at the physiatrist's lack of attention (we haven't heard a word from him since he visited Henry in the hospital), worried about the future. Should I have taken Henry to a medical center where they might have had experience with this sort of thing? Why didn't I contact that place in Atlanta— where Mike's high school friend, who became a quadriplegic after an automobile accident, was taken? Mike and I even visited him there. I *knew* about that place and their innovative work with spinal cord injuries.

And what about other rehab places? Was I negligent in not pursuing care at a place that specializes in Henry's problem, regardless of where in the country that might be? I keep looking back and seeing my mistakes. I wonder what I'm getting wrong now.

40

When Henry and I look back, our only regret is that we didn't have three, four, even five children. We're the kind of parents who would have loved a houseful of kids—all that chirping, laughing, fighting, crying, all those bare feet, the way children turn you outside of yourself. When Laurie and Mike were growing older and our life was quieting into a new one, we asked ourselves, over and over: *Now, why did we stop at two?*

So it wasn't surprising, back when Laurie and Bob had their twins in August 2002, that Henry and I moved in with them. We'd planned to stay one month, but at the end of the month, I didn't think they were ready to go it alone. Henry, on the other hand, felt it was time. "Laurie wouldn't leave me in a fix like this," I told him. "How can I leave her?"

We stayed on for two more months, spending less and less time there, more and more time back home, beginning with overnights, then two-day weekends, four-day weekends, eventually weaning Laurie and Bob off us, weaning us off those sweet babies.

The first month, the girls slept in a Pack 'n Play

upstairs in our room. We wanted Laurie to get her sleep, since she was recuperating from a caesarian and nursing two infants. Neither Lucy nor Zoe would take a bottle, which meant Laurie was nursing nonstop. We also wanted Bob to get his sleep, because after a long day at work, he jumped into fatherly duties the minute he walked in the door.

Every few hours during the night, Henry or I would change one baby, bring her downstairs to Laurie, keep Laurie company in the nursery while she nursed, chatting with her about this new life of hers or reading aloud to her from the stack of how-to-care-for-an-infant books she kept beside the nursing chair. Then back upstairs to burp the baby and rock her to sleep. Some nights Henry and I would pass each other on the stairs, bringing one baby down to nurse, taking the other back up. Once, after I'd woken Laurie and we'd settled ourselves in the nursery for her to nurse and me to read aloud, she pulled the blanket away from the little rosy face and said, "Oh, Mom, I just nursed this one!"

Sometimes, when the babies were fussy, Henry and I would take them outside to the slatted swing hanging from the beadboard ceiling on the front porch. We'd let the night pour cool on all of us. I wondered what Margaret and Linda, neighbors across the street, might think if they cracked open a window at three in the morning and saw the four of us swinging, heard Henry singing "Take Me Out to the Ballgame," or me, "Let Me Call You Sweetheart."

•

My sister, Brenda, used to tell her four sons that the decision whom to marry was the most important they would make in their lives. Which means Henry and I were nuts to commit to a person we knew only slightly better than some stranger we might share an elevator with in a tall building. During our superfast glide into marriage, there was no way I could know that he would be irresistibly drawn—as I was—to parenthood. And grandparenthood. Our marriage became a giant testament to intuition. To luck. Time cut us a good deal. What matters deeply to me matters deeply to him. We could not have predicted that our future would find us lying flat on our backs in a bed in our married daughter's house, each holding a fretful baby on our chest, patting them, rolling our hands a little from place to place as if there were some secret spot we could touch to help them be done with their crying. Couldn't have predicted that we'd turn to each other in the dark and grin, struck blind by our good fortune.

41

Henry can pee on his own! No more cathing! We feel like taking out a full-page ad in *The Charlotte Observer*, plastering the news on a billboard beside I-85: CHARLOTTE MAN PEES LIKE CRAZY! Instead, we celebrate with a candlelight dinner on the screened porch. The air is warm, the sky navy. Every now and then, a breeze rolls in. We have gazpacho and a salad with shrimp, arugula, avocado, mango, snow peas, and mint. A lemony dressing. Henry opens a pinot grigio. Just before I hand him my glass to fill, he reaches across the table, takes my face in his hand. His lips brush my cheek.

"Thank you, sweetie," he says, "for everything you do."

"Thank *you* for everything *you* do," I say, laughingly. "All that great peeing."

I push back my chair, a musical scrape on the brick floor. I lean over him and hug his neck.

·

Next morning, Sunday, I see that the swelling has traveled farther up his right leg. I leave a message on the rehab doctor's line, asking if a doctor on call will get back to me. A nurse phones to say there are no doctors on call over the weekend. She says they have them available for their inpatients but not their outpatients.

"That's hard to believe," I say. My peppery voice.

"Yes," she says, "we've had a lot of complaints about this from other patients. You'll just have to take your husband to the emergency room."

I don't want to take him to the emergency room. But maybe I should. The back and forth in my head, like a gong.

I decide to gamble and wait until tomorrow. Maybe he can see a doctor then. Maybe no harm will be done by waiting. But what doctor will we call?

.

First thing Monday morning, I call Jim, the neurologist who visited us in the hospital. I leave a message, and in less than an hour, he returns my call. Not the receptionist. Not his nurse. Jim. I ask if he'll be Henry's doctor and follow him now. He says yes, of course, and after I describe Henry's swollen leg, he sends us for an ultrasound.

.

The technician is moving the little probe over Henry's leg. She's silent, her eyes on the screen. My eyes are on that lavishly bright screen, too, studying, trying to decipher the violent splashes of red. *Pay attention,* I tell myself. *You can read this ultrasound. Just concentrate. There. See that spot the tech keeps going over and over? Probably not a good sign.*

Then a loud ring. The phone on the desk behind my chair. The tech scoots her stool back, reaches around me, picks up. It's Jim. The doctor! Calling for results while Henry is still on the table! I can hardly believe his attentiveness.

There are two blood clots in his right leg.

Jim sends us directly to the hospital. Not the same one we were in before. A different one. We live close to the three major hospitals in Charlotte. Don't know if that's something to brag about or not.

Because Jim called ahead, check-in at the hospital is smooth.

And then we're alone in Henry's room. I'm worried about these clots, but Henry seems unfazed. In fact, he looks a little disoriented. In a bit of a trance. Floating above the events occurring down here. I wonder what he's thinking. In the past, of course, we would have discussed every piece of this new development. But we've been a little outside of normal for a while now.

42

I'm dying to ring for a nurse or aide, get things started. But I force myself to wait. *Give them time,* I tell myself.

An hour goes by.

I hit the button. "Could someone come to the room, please?"

A nurse bursts through the door. He's a too-tall, spindly guy with a full head of black hair, and he's pulsing with nervous energy. He's mostly arms and legs.

"Where did you come from?" he shrieks. "How did you get here? What's your name?" He spins Henry's hospital bracelet until he can read the name. "Why are you here?"

Henry sees me hardening and signals me with his eyes not to respond. He's going to handle this. *Good. More like himself. Normal.* When he speaks, his voice is clear, unruffled, and polite: "Well, first, have you had a chance to look at my chart?"

The nurse says he has not. In word spasms that leave him winded, he tells us he's going to go do that right now.

"Thank you," Henry says. "Thank you."

"Call me Peter," he says.

"Thank you, Peter," Henry says.

But he has already speed-walked out the door.

.

After an hour or so, he darts back in, full tilt, and hands Henry a printed apology card. What exactly is the hospital apologizing for? Ignoring our arrival? Employing a manic nurse? He also hands me a "gift"—a coffee mug with the hospital logo trailing around its middle. Will I really enjoy recalling this hospital stay while sipping my morning coffee? He's going on and on about not being told a new patient was on his floor, how did this happen, how long were we here before he discovered us? He adds that he hasn't had a chance to check Henry's chart.

I need to go home and get Henry's things. But there's no way I'll leave him now.

.

Early evening, Jim, the neurologist, comes to see Henry, says he will start Lovenox, blood-thinning injections.

.

Hours later, late evening, no Lovenox.

I buzz the nurses' station. "Is it time for my husband's Lovenox yet?"

A voice answers that our nurse will be with us shortly.

Peter pops his head in to say there are no orders for Lovenox. Seems odd that it wouldn't be started right away.

.

Next morning, Jim comes by and is shocked to hear they have not given Henry Lovenox. He specifically wrote orders.

With each hour that passes, Henry seems to grow weaker. The mattress is thin, lumpy, and narrow, and he can't find a comfortable position. The room is tiny. Not a table or a chair for my jacket, handbag, book, Tupperware lunch. We ask Peter if there's a larger room available. He says we must pay $52.50 out-of-pocket extra per day for a larger room. I ask about the many vacant rooms on the floor that are larger. He replies, "A room is a room is a room! They're all the same size, except for the suites on the seventh floor, and those cost extra."

Another nurse, not assigned to us, comes into the room while Peter is explaining about paying for a larger room. After Peter leaves, she tells me to pick which vacant room I'd like; she'll move us to that one.

"I don't know why they tell people they have to pay for a larger room," she says, "when larger rooms are available right here on the floor."

That so gracious a person would enter our lives at

this moment is almost more than I can bear. "Thank you," I manage to say. I shut my eyes to hold back the tears. She sees, and puts her arms around me. She's large and soft and smells like peppermint.

Henry is moved within the hour.

Later, when I take a walk down the hall, I notice that our original room is now a supply closet. The door is ajar and I see mops, buckets, brooms. I concentrate on keeping the soles of my shoes in firm contact with the floor. *Just forget it,* I tell myself. *Suck in your stomach and keep walking. Don't stop at the nurses' station. Don't say anything smart-alecky to Peter. Concentrate on the lovely nurse who moved us.*

It's so hard to know what's important and worth fighting about, and what I need to just let be.

.

Even in our new room, I'm constantly retucking the bottom sheet on Henry's bed, pulling the top sheet tight and smooth, and folding it back over the blanket. I organize, then reorganize the room. Now I'm moving the trash can to the corner, pushing the smaller of the two chairs into the spot the trash can occupied. As though everything depends on these little rituals. When I look up, I see that expression on his face, the one I call flinty. I stop my organizing. Go over to him.

"I just feel depressed," he says. He's on his back, the bed rolled flat, his face turned toward me. I see the beginnings of a stubble. "I'm worried about losing

all this time not being in physical therapy. What happened to the first three weeks being so important?"

The way he sounds—so plaintive, so wronged—
makes my breathing go shallow.

I throw his covers back and lie down next to him,
pull the covers over both of us, curve myself around
him, feel the warmth of his chest, hold on with everything I have. The bed is really not wide enough for
two people, but we stay like this for a long time, all
shoulders and elbows.

43

Dreams are usually dim, unclear, and forgettable, as though written in smoke. Even as you're starting to recall them, they're beginning to fade. But this one stays clear and won't let me go. For days afterward, I keep having to remind myself that it was, in fact, a dream, not real.

.

We're having friends over for a party. Everyone is milling around in the den. Four guys from Terminix are also here for our quarterly pest inspection. I'm frustrated that I don't have time to supervise them, so I practically command the one who's in charge, "You can look around the house, but do not, under any circumstances, spray inside. If you see a problem, check with me before you do anything."

The guy nods okay, and he and his coworkers head up the stairs.

After a while, I notice that Henry's gone. I leave our company to go look for him.

I find him with the Terminix men in the upstairs

guest room where our grandchildren sleep when they spend the night. The workmen are coating the frames of the windows and doors with powdery white insecticide, circling the room with their spray guns, spraying it—thick—everywhere, even outlining the twin beds with poison. With all the spraying, the room has taken on the color of snow.

"Why didn't you call me?" I scream at the guys. I'm so angry I'm trembling. (I'll still be trembling when I wake up.)

The first one shrugs. I shoot my question at each guy, but nobody answers. Finally, the one in charge tilts his head toward Henry, as if to explain they didn't call me because Henry gave them the go-ahead.

There's a large, cleaverlike weapon lying on the floor. I pick it up. Whom shall I use it on?

Suddenly, I realize what I'm doing. I'm horrified.

Gingerly, but quickly, I lay it back down.

Then I spot a jug of red wine. I want everyone to know how angry I am, so I grab the jug by the neck with both hands and sling it across the room. The bed Henry and I sleep in downstairs suddenly appears in this upstairs room. Jagged glass and gushes of wine—or is it blood?—all over our creamy down comforter. Now look what I've done.

·

You don't have to look far for an interpretation of this dream. It's that same feeling that I alone am responsible. It will take fierce determination on my part and a brain that never goes on automatic to steer this ship, put it on an easy, bright course, bring my husband safely back to shore.

Part of me is dead tired from having to be so responsible, and part of me feels that I have reason (good reason) not to hand over the responsibility to anyone. Not even Henry.

I have to admit, being in charge feels, in some ways, like an ascendancy. As though I'm suddenly six feet tall. A world-class expert. I hear myself telling friends self-aggrandizing stories of how I stopped some nurse from giving Henry the wrong pill, requested a test that ended up providing useful information, refused treatment, suggested treatment, got an appointment—a thousand different instances in which my quick thinking kept him from further harm. As though I'm in the running for some major prize for alertness.

The hard part, though, is that at the same time I'm feeling I'm the only smart one around here, I'm also terrified of misjudging a situation, making a wrong decision, bringing ruin.

And.

I'm furious.

Furious with the physiatrist. How dare he let this happen to my husband and then vanish!

And I'm not just furious with the physiatrist. I'm furious with everybody who has done anything wrong these past weeks, or has come close to doing anything wrong. Oh, and I get to judge what's wrong and what's not wrong.

I'm even furious with Henry. He's the one who made the decision to have the epidural. Forget the fact that, at the time, I thought it was a good idea. I'm too busy thinking if I can't trust him to make good decisions, I can't trust anyone. I'll just elbow my way in to make all the decisions. Which also makes me furious.

44

Henry is clean-shaven, teeth brushed, hair combed, ready to change out of his hospital gown into the sweat-pants and T-shirt I've brought from home. Discharge day, nine in the morning, five days since admittance. His prothrombin time (how long it takes blood to clot, measured by a blood test) is regulated now. He'll take a blood thinner to keep it in check.

Jim comes to the room. Henry and I assume he's here to sign the papers and send us on our way. Instead, he tells us he's so sorry, but Henry's pro time is too low and they'll have to check it again this after-noon. Jim feels that he can be discharged then. We're disappointed, but it will be only a few extra hours.

Early afternoon, Jim comes in again and tells Henry yes, he can go home. His numbers are fine. Henry is so relieved. I see him draw his hand across his cheek. Is he about to cry?

But then Jim has a second thought: Wait. Let him just double-check with the pharmacy to make sure it's safe for Henry to be discharged.

"I'll be right back," he says.

Henry and I wait. I wonder if I should go ahead and start helping him into his clothes, get a head start moving toward home. I decide to wait. Jim will be back soon. We can still get home in time for dinner. Lentil soup, made last night, is in the refrigerator.

Jim walks into the room. His face is pinkish with emotion. The seconds move slowly. We're waiting for him to speak. I glance at Henry. The head of the bed is rolled up, a pillow doubled behind his neck.

In a low, sad voice, Jim says that since the Lovenox was started a day late, the pharmacist thinks Henry should be on it a *full* five days before being discharged. He shouldn't go home until tomorrow morning.

This is not Jim's fault. He's a neurologist; he does not normally deal with blood clots. He's doing us a big favor taking care of Henry. And anyway, he left orders. Those orders just weren't followed.

Henry's body goes limp as the ground beneath him shifts yet again. I want to reach over and steady him. Pat his arm. Shoot, I'd steady the ground if I knew how.

45

"You can do it, Dad," Laurie said, patting his arm, laughing her big laugh. Henry had picked a card from the deck, read it, then fell back in his chair in mock horror. He was now cracking up, laughing *his* big laugh. (The two of them and their big laughs.)

Henry, Laurie, Mike, and I were at the kitchen table playing Pictionary. It was one of those rare Friday nights when neither child (both teenagers) had plans. No school football or basketball game. No movie. No friends over. When they were little and always around, Henry and I had no idea that the time the four of us spent together would dwindle. We probably thought everything would remain what it had been. The places where life happened would never change.

Laurie and Henry were partners. Mike and I were partners. We always had the same partners for Pictionary; it was the only way to even things up. Laurie and I are really good artists. Mike and Henry are pretty bad.

Mike turned the little hourglass over. Henry

picked up his Sharpie and started. He drew a few swirly lines, stopped, turned the square of paper counterclockwise, drew again, adjusted his glasses as though that would turn him into an artist, pulled back to assess what he'd done, drew some more, slapped his pen down on the table in a gesture of finality, and slid his drawing over to Laurie.

"Done," he said.

Laurie, across from me and next to Henry, looked at his picture. Mike, on my right, leaned around me to see. I could almost feel how badly Laurie and Mike wanted their dad's drawing to be something recognizable.

Laurie, whose job it was to guess what her partner had drawn, only said, "Uh-*huh*."

I was trying to decide whether she knew right away what it was or she was buying time.

"Uh-*huh*," she said again.

Buying time.

The sand was flowing through the hourglass.

"A helicopter?" she finally guessed.

"*Helicopter?*" Henry said, incredulous. "*Helicopter?* How did you get *helicopter?*"

"Well, then, what is it?" she asked. She gave the paper a little turn.

"It's Los Angeles," he said.

"Los Angeles?" Laurie, Mike, and I all said at the exact same moment. Then the four of us started laughing so hard we could've choked.

"Wait, wait!" Henry wiped his eyes under his glasses, took the paper from Laurie. "I'm going to show you how it's Los Angeles."

He held the paper up. We were all studying it.

"See this? It's an outline of the United States. A map." He traced with his finger a shape that *could* be interpreted as America, but it would be a stretch.

"And see this?" He was pointing to a long, skinny shape inside the larger shape. "That's California." Then he pointed to a dot inside the long, skinny shape. "And this is Los Angeles."

The dot didn't exactly look like a city, and the scalloped shape it was located in didn't exactly look like a state. But for the four of us that night, under the steady light from the brass fixture over the pine table, it could have been the exact center of the universe. Give or take an inch.

.

Just an ordinary moment. Nothing really makes this memory stand out. Like so many of our memories that are only little half-stories, mere routine, silly dailiness. Why do we tell them over and over, trotting them out for friends and even people we barely know? We turn to the man next to us on the airplane, the one trying to read his book, and tell about the time our family played Pictionary. We mention to the checkout girl in Laurel Market that we spent three months at our daughter and son-in-law's house helping to take care of their newborn twins. Is it because we love what these stories say about us, the rosy image they project, exactly what we'd hoped and imagined our lives would be? *Look at this wonderful family I created!* This explanation embarrasses me. But I have to admit there's some truth to it. Also true: When the present presses in so hard we can't imagine a future, the past hints at a larger order and shows us why and how we'll move forward. It can be like a map.

46

I call Henry the minute I wake up. He's coming home today! "Good morning!" I say. If my voice were something you could see, it would be shimmering.

His voice is weak and whispery. "I've been sick all night. Come as fast as you can."

He is not telling me to take my time. He is not saying don't rush, he's fine. The things he usually would say.

I can't get to the hospital fast enough. The car jerks all the way there, like a bumper car, fast, then slow, because I can't stop my leg from shaking.

.

I push open the door to his room. He's sitting on the side of the bed, head bowed, eyes on his upturned hands in his lap, legs dangling. The door to the bathroom is open. I see Beth, a smart, young aide who's been assigned to us before, standing at the toilet, emptying one of those plastic basins you vomit in. She comes back into the room, swishes the little basin out in the sink, places it in Henry's hands. Peter, the nurse, is beside the window, one elbow resting on the sill.

I sit down beside Henry on the bed, my jacket still on, handbag strap over my shoulder. I drape a protective arm around him. He whispers he's been sick all night.

I feel *my* stomach going sour.

Now Beth says she needs to take his temperature. He barely lifts his head, so she stoops a little to slip the thermometer under his tongue.

"What is it?" I ask.

"One hundred and three," she says.

Before I can react, Peter walks over to her and asks if she went out last night. She makes a point of not answering him. She concentrates on filling in a chart, lets her long, honey-colored hair fall over her face. She even twists a little so that her back is to him.

I start to say something. *Do you think my husband could be getting dehydrated? I mean, since he was sick all night? And this high fever?* is what I want to ask.

But Peter talks over me, circling to position himself right in front of Beth. His voice is flirty—also, speeded up. "Did you have a big date? Oh, yeah, I bet you had a big date!"

Beth ignores him; she's not going to join in. He doesn't give up. The loud, cheeky remarks keep coming.

·

Later I walk down the hall and see Peter lounging across the bed in the vacant room next door, watching a soap opera on TV.

.

Beth, in our room again, says that if I feel uncomfortable with Peter, I can request a different nurse.

"How?" I ask.

"Just call the nursing supervisor," she says. "Patients do it all the time."

I feel that, without saying too much, she's trying to get across just how inept Peter is.

Once again, someone in the hospital sticks her neck out for us. "Thank you, Beth," I say, my voice lifting in gratitude. "Thank you. Thank you." Maybe I say it four times.

"I would hope someone would do this for my parents," she says. She's probably the same age as our kids.

.

I call the nursing supervisor, request a change, am careful not to criticize Peter, use Beth's tactful phrasing and say only that I'd feel more comfortable with a different nurse.

No problem, the supervisor replies. She'll assign him to another room and a different nurse to ours. Even though I feel bad for the patient who's getting him, I'm hugely relieved.

Our new nurse, Ann, has a lipsticked mouth, but I can barely take in the rest of her face because she will not look directly at me. She challenges everything I say. When I ask for ice because Henry's mouth is so dry and maybe he'll be able to tolerate a few chips on his tongue, she says in a growly voice that there's plenty of water in my husband's pitcher and she'll get him ice when she can, but it's not like he doesn't have anything to drink.

Did the nursing supervisor tell Peter I asked for a different nurse? Are Ann and Peter friends?

I wonder if I'm becoming paranoid.

I wish we could just go home.

Henry is unaware of the drama. Now I regret replacing Peter. I should have left well enough alone. I take charge, and what do I do? Mess everything up. For a brief moment, I think of the physiatrist. How he tried to make Henry better, but things turned out worse. Now I've done the same thing. If only I could take this quick realization and turn it into a full forgiveness of the physiatrist. But, too fast, I'm sucked back into this room.

Mike comes. He cannot believe Ann's hostility. Now she won't even answer me—or Mike—when we speak to her. He says he'll stay, for sure, until the shift changes.

·

Mike and I sit side by side, next to the bed. We watch Henry so closely, we could tell you the exact second his eyelids flutter.

I ask Mike how he's doing with all that's going on.

He tells me he dreams nonstop—awful nightmares—about running into the physiatrist.

"Are you saying you don't want to ever see him again?" I ask.

"No, I *want* to see him. When I used to wheel Dad around the floor in the hospital and then in rehab, I was always hoping I'd turn the corner and run into the physiatrist in the hall. And then I pictured myself just—well, hurting him." He stops and waits for my reaction. I look at his face. I think he's embarrassed by what he just said.

"You know I'm not a physical person," he says. "Never have been. But I keep dreaming of doing harm to that doctor."

"Oh, Mike" is all I can say. But I'm thinking I hate this dark enfolding him, hate his fitful sleep, hate that my sweet-tempered son feels hate.

"I'm not sad," he says. "I'm not even worried. I'm *angry.* I feel like this whole thing that happened to Dad has changed me in a major way. Maybe it's just that I've grown up. I catch on now to what can happen. But really, it's not a positive change. I've developed an anger I never had before. And I don't know what to do with it."

I can almost hear bees buzzing inside my skull. The sound of a family being invaded and overtaken.

·

Mid-afternoon, Beth checks Henry's vitals. Temperature still sky-high. Blood pressure has now dropped. Very low. She'll check back in a little while.

Ann comes in with two blood pressure medications. I tell her that since his last reading was so low, maybe he shouldn't take these. She glares at me. I glare back. Still holding the little paper cup of pills, she wheels around and leaves the room.

Mike stands, calls out to her in a stern voice I hardly recognize, "Just wait a minute!" But she's gone. I touch his arm. He sits back down beside me and breaks into a smile I do know quite well. "I think I'll focus my anger on her now!" he says.

We don't move from Henry's bedside. Not until after midnight, when we both finally leave.

.

Next morning, I get to the hospital early. Henry is better. Nausea gone. Temperature normal. But his blood pressure is now high. I buzz the nurses' station and ask if he should take his blood pressure meds.

Ann pokes her head in the room and says she thought I didn't want my husband to have any blood pressure medication. I try to explain. She cuts me off, says she's busy, then she's gone. I can see she's not going to bring any blood pressure meds into this room.

Around noon, Jim comes. I'm so happy to see him, I could knock him down with a hug. He gets the blood pressure medication for Henry, names the hospital infection he contracted (lost to me in the flurry of information), gives us prescriptions for an antibiotic and blood thinner, signs the discharge papers.

I pull out of the parking deck, hand my ticket to

the woman in the booth, smile, pay, *thank you,* swing around to pick up Henry, waiting for me in a wheelchair at the entrance. He and a transporter, an older man, slightly built, are deep in conversation. The transporter helps him into the front seat. Click of the seat belt. I pull away from the curb, slip between cars picking up patients, dropping off visitors. Head for Scotland Avenue, home.

As I drive through Charlotte's leafy streets, the broad oaks, this sunstruck afternoon, what comes to me, what I find myself repeating over and over in my head: *Okay. We can do this.*

47

One mid-winter trip to New York, after a Broadway matinee, Henry and I walked out of the theater into a sudden snowstorm. The flakes were so soft, so beautiful, it looked as though all of Manhattan were an outdoor stage, lit up. We glided serenely for blocks, hugging each other, snow tipping our eyelashes. We walked from the theater district over to Fifth Avenue, then turned toward uptown, passing the shining store windows that lined the street in those years. When we got to a Spanish leather store, Henry stopped.

"Wait," he said, "let's go in." He had hoped to buy a leather jacket on this trip, but everywhere we'd gone—Bloomingdale's, the shops in SoHo, the Village—they'd been too expensive.

"Are you kidding?" I said. "Those jackets will cost a million dollars!"

"I know. But let's just look. For the hell of it."

We ducked inside the bright, starry store. A tall, elegant woman with a melodic foreign accent—French, maybe? Belgian?—greeted us. She had well-cut dark hair that moved when she moved. Her sleeveless silk blouse and narrow wool skirt looked expensive. So did her shoes. Impossibly high heels. Henry told her he was interested in a jacket. She curved her manicured forefinger slightly to lead us back.

There were very few leather jackets hanging, but she lifted out one, a deep brown. She helped Henry out of his L.L.Bean canvas car coat and into the jacket, a smooth action, Henry's coat now over her delicate, bare arm, the new jacket now skimming his back. The leather—I could tell from just looking—was as fine as the skin of chocolate pudding.

I also could tell that Henry had, just in the past minutes, become an expert on the *how* of how wealthy people shop. He turned from side to side to admire himself in the three-way mirror, slid his hands deep in the pockets, then out. He tugged discriminatingly at the lapels. Buttoned a button. Rolled back his shoulders and lengthened his neck.

The saleswoman dropped his car coat on a chair, stepped closer to him, placed both hands on those ample shoulders, adjusted the leather jacket ever so slightly. Another thing I could tell: She was an expert on the *how* of how to sell an expensive jacket to wealthy people.

But then. In the middle of this divine choreography. Breaking this expensive silence. Henry released a fart. A bomb. Long. And slow. And loud. As if that jacket freed him from everything. Except embarrassment.

I heard it. For sure, the saleswoman heard it.

Henry looked at me. I looked at him. We were both so mortified, all we could do was laugh. We couldn't stop. Tears ran down our faces. We'd been playing at being grown up. Playing at being wealthy. The only bad thing that could possibly happen was a brief betrayal by a digestive tract.

Henry unbuttoned the jacket, peeled it off, placed it on the chair, grabbed his car coat, neither of us saying a word. I sensed the saleswoman just standing there. I could not look her in the face.

Henry and I fell over each other trying to get out of there, our laughter breaking loose, like something that had no business being in such a place.

48

Henry seems more tired than usual. Mostly he just wants to lie on the sofa with his legs propped on a pillow and wait for the next hour to roll in.

I'm tired, too. And I don't feel like cooking, so I drive over to Price's Chicken Coop to pick up dinner. There's a line of customers out the door and onto the sidewalk. But because the air is thick with the crispy promise of fried chicken, everyone is jovial. Construction workers in overalls, bank execs in subdued ties, suburban moms holding babies—a cozy coexistence of people who understand that the ordinary becomes extraordinary in a vat of oil.

Those of us waiting to place an order at the counter angle sideways to allow satisfied customers already served to ease back through the crowd, out the glass doors, carrying their soggy paper bags or cardboard boxes of legs, thighs, breasts, livers. What's going on around me lifts me. I'm that desperate for a lift.

.

At the kitchen table, Henry runs his tongue over his lips. I lick my fingertip and press it to the golden crumbs scattered on my place mat, then to my mouth.

Since Henry's epidural, I could eat fried chicken all day every day and not gain a pound. I could consume bags of potato chips, multiple Heath bars, milkshakes, doughnuts, and not only would I not gain, I'd actually lose. The pounds melt off. My face is thinner than ever. My looping despair seems to have an appetite all its own, gobbling away at me. The assault on Henry's body is an assault on mine. I haven't weighed this little since college.

49

Every time Henry or I took a trip without the other—I might be teaching a workshop in Atlanta, he might be traveling with his college pals to see the University of Florida play for a national championship—we left little notes for each other. We worked hard at finding more and more creative places to leave our notes. If I was the one traveling, he tucked his note between the sweaters in my suitcase. If he was traveling, I hid my note in the toe of his rolled-up sock. If I was staying home, he wrapped his around my toothbrush in the medicine cabinet. If he was staying, I taped mine to the half and half carton in the fridge.

Hey Sweetie—

Who's going to tell me to drink more water? Who's going to tell me I should get more sleep? How am I going to make it through these next few days without you? Oh brother! Anyway, darling—I hope you have a great trip. Don't worry about me or anything else for the next few days. You are one in a million and I love you so much.

Hank

Hey, Hen! I'll miss you. I think I always feel a little kerflooey when we separate. But I'll see you Sunday night. And I thank my lucky stars I got you!

Love, love and more love,

Judy

Does it count as "going away" if it's less than 25 miles? I think it does, so here's my travel note for you. I hope you have a good time at the workshop. I'm glad you're getting away.

I love you, Sweetie,

Hank

Quick—before you come to the bedroom to get your suitcase—I have to write this!! I hope you have so much fun with your ole' pals. I can hear the jokes, all the ribbing that will go on, and I know you'll be happy. Hope the Gators kill whoever they're playing! (Football, right?) GO, GATORS! CHOMP! CHOMP! I love you so much & am really glad you're taking this trip. I'll see your sweet face on Monday.

Judy

Hey Sweetie—

I'm sure going to miss lying next to you tonight. I promise I'll be back in my regular spot soon. You are wonderful and I love you so much. I'm definitely the lucky one.

Hank

We'll make it through all this—I promise! I really think we've got something very special. I love you so much, and I'm sorry I have a lot of rough edges right now.

Love you,
Judy

Sweetie—
You're leaving in a few minutes and I'm thinking about how cute you look and how much I like you and want to let you know. See you tomorrow night.
Hank

Here's what I want to tell you: You're the nicest person I've ever met. For sure, I'm the lucky one.
I love you,
Judy

Hey Sweetie—
I'm so happy you're doing this mini-vacation with your girlfriends. I worry, though, y'all are going to run out of things to talk about. (Ha!) I'll see you on Friday.
I love you—Hank
P.S. Think about trying the kayak.

I save his notes in my rolltop desk. He keeps mine in the drawer of his bedside table. Those scraps of paper like silver confetti.

50

Think about trying the kayak.

That note was obviously written early in our relationship. Before he knew me very well. Before he understood there's no way I would just up and make a decision to go kayaking.

We all, in the beginning, think we can train our spouses. Turn them into versions of ourselves.

I remember when Mother's older sister, Aunt Emma, seventy-six and widowed, was about to marry her second husband, Ernie. Aunt Emma confided to me that she hated the thin, pastel, short-sleeved shirts he wore. "But after we're married," she whispered, "I'll get him to dress better."

After we're married, Judy will take to kayaking.

51

Night after night, Henry's "good" leg has been jerking, as though the nerve endings in that leg are
misfiring. The spasms seize his whole body. I can
actually see the spasms through our down comforter,
a trembling like Jell-O. Every fifteen seconds, another
spasm. I can't tell whether they're keeping me awake
or *I'm* keeping me awake. Why do I lie here, timing
the spasms, counting silently? Do I believe watching
will stop them? Like when I used to tell my children
I could end their hiccups just by staring them in the
face, waiting with exaggerated anticipation for the
next one. Or like the wart on Laurie's tiny hand that,
at bedtime, night after night, she and I, with great
patience, wished away.

We see Jim, who suggests a muscle relaxant.
Henry doesn't want to take another medication. Jim
understands.

Henry and I are side by side in chairs across from
him. He leans closer, pulls off his wire-rimmed glasses
with one hand, squeezes the bridge of his nose with
the other, slides his glasses back on. His expression

is benevolent. I think he's probably going to ask how physical therapy is going, how our kids are, something friendly like that.

"How are you *doing*, Henry?" he asks, his face forming a question more probing than his actual words. Then his words match his face: "Emotionally, I mean."

Immediately, Henry's eyes get red and watery. Then he's openly crying, which, I can tell, is a relief and an embarrassment at the same time. Jim does not appear surprised. He passes a tissue box.

Henry's crying lasts only seconds, and then he tries to wipe his face of all emotion. His cheeks are still wet, though. He answers Jim's question. Jim is empathetic, understands, explains about depression and serotonin. Which leads to a recommendation of Zoloft. Again, Henry is reluctant to add another med. With no urgency or pressure, Jim tells why he thinks an antidepressant is a good idea. Unusual for him to push, even to this gentle degree.

Henry has so much trust in him that he finally says yes. I'm glad. Not only do I trust Jim implicitly, but I see Henry as depressed much of the time now. I can read his mind: *If only I could do the ordinary things I used to do, roll the garbage to the curb, change the recessed bulb in the kitchen ceiling, ride my bike, play tennis, racquetball. Not be an old man.*

52

My own private list of if-onlys:

1. If only Henry had not seen the ad in the paper for the physiatrist.
2. If only he'd tried acupuncture instead.
3. Or physical therapy.
4. Or biofeedback.
5. Reflexology.
6. Meditation.
7. Massage.
8. If only he'd decided, *Well, I have back pain, but I can live with it. I'll just skip the epidural.* It's not that he's a complainer. It's just that he's a person who believes there's a medical procedure for every ill. I'm more willing to watch and wait, try alternatives. I believe each time we sign on for an invasive procedure, we're rolling the dice.
9. If only I'd tried to *talk him into* acupuncture, physical therapy, biofeedback, reflexology, meditation, massage, or maybe just living with the pain.
10. If only I'd been called back to wait with him before

the epidural. Would that have slowed down—or speeded up—the process? If Henry had had the epidural five minutes earlier or five minutes later, if we could just go back to that exact moment and do one thing differently, could we rewrite the story?

53

Every August, since the children were young, Henry and I have taken them to the beach for a week. When Mike and Laurie were in high school and college, they brought friends. Sometimes they invited a boyfriend or girlfriend. Eventually, those romantic interests became family—Mike married Brooke; Laurie married Bob. Then came Lucy and Zoe, then Tess. (Later, Mike and Brooke's son, Benjamin.)

For years, we rented the same side of a duplex in Wrightsville Beach. After the epidural, I decided we needed a different house, one with a shorter dock leading out to the beach. I researched online, explored places in North and South Carolina, called realty companies, found the perfect house. On Oak Island. Four bedrooms. Oceanfront. Short dock.

All spring and summer, following the epidural, the six of us looked forward to our August beach trip, as though we'd had the breath knocked out of us, but we knew the salt air would help us breathe easy again.

.

Henry rides with Bob. I ride with Laurie, Lucy, and Zoe. Mike, Brooke, and Tess get to the house a little before the rest of us, having picked up the keys from the rental agency. Lucy and Zoe immediately snap open their matching princess suitcases; toss their shorts, T-shirts, and pajamas across the living room rug; find their bathing suits and scramble into them. They start begging Brooke to get Tess's suit on, putting every ounce of themselves toward the effort. But Brooke and Mike, Laurie and Bob, Henry and I are huddled together, in the far corner of the living room, staring at what I had not bargained for, what I had not noticed in the description of the house, what the realtor failed to mention: a narrow, steep, black iron spiral staircase leading from the main level down to the master bedroom, where Henry and I will sleep.

In these rented rooms overlooking that big sea, everything feels suddenly strange. We were not fully at ease at home, but at least it was our *familiar* ill-at-ease. Here, there's—well, there's that spiral staircase. Someone must help Henry up the steps in the morning, then back down at night. He goes first—a step, pause, another step, a slight teeter, regain balance. We're right behind him, guiding his elbow, holding on to the waist of his shorts. Between these slow, halting trips, if he needs anything from our bedroom, we get it for him.

I should feel grateful having the children under our same roof. They definitely take some of the burden off me. I see Laurie pouring Grape-Nuts and slicing a banana for Henry's breakfast, while he waits at the table. Mike brings his computer over: "Pop, take a look. You'll like this." I see different ones at different times staying in from the beach to keep him company.

But I'm alert to every nuance of his behavior. The staircase is not the only problem. He's having trouble falling asleep at night, because of the spasms in his good leg. Since he's up much of the night, he can't rouse himself in the morning. He sleeps till noon, or later. After that, he sits on the sofa. Only twice during the week does he venture out on the beach. The dock is rough and uneven, the sand beyond the dock deep and difficult to plow through. He says the sun feels prickly on his bad leg.

Mike and I take a walk down the beach and have a private chat. Laurie and I whisper in the kitchen. We talk about their dad. They give me advice. I *yes, but* them. Then I stop *yes, but*ting and listen. *Have you tried this? That?* I take in their advice, ask for more. As though the three of us are coparenting their dad. Our conversations turn into a muffled brooding. Which then turns into an almost obsessive nostalgia for the past.

After a couple days, we find a safe place to rest: We give in to our desire to go back in time. One night, after the little ones are in bed, we grown-ups—the six of us—remain around the table long after dinner, Henry and me telling stories from long ago, those memories like life preservers we throw to one another.

At one point, Henry looks at me; I look at him. Okay, our glances say, now's the time to tell:

In the late seventies, Henry and I left Laurie and Mike with my parents in Rock Hill and drove to Blowing Rock for the weekend, a tidy stash of marijuana in my purse. We'd smoked once before with friends, and they'd left a Baggie with us.

Our first night, driving to dinner, we smoked a joint. By the time we got to the restaurant, ironically called the Smoke Tree Lodge, we were both as high as Grandfather Mountain. The restaurant had a soup and salad buffet, but Henry and I, in our bobbling state, could not figure out how to work it. We finally decided that the tiny white ceramic cups were for salad (even though they were stacked beside the kettle of soup). All we could stuff into those miniature bowls was a piece of lettuce, a cherry tomato, a crouton. When the waiter came to our table to take our order for dinner, he stared at our "salad cups." Then he looked from the cups to Henry to me. I looked at Henry. He looked at me. We both looked at our cups. It suddenly came clear what we'd done—and we started laughing uncontrollably, almost like a coughing fit. The waiter stared, we laughed. He asked if we had decided on an entrée. We laughed. I'm not sure how many minutes passed before he finally drifted away. We just sat there, crying with laughter.

"I knew it! I knew it!" Laurie screams with joy. "There was no way Dad could make it through the seventies without smoking pot! Mom, I wasn't so sure about you, but I knew Dad wouldn't miss out on that!"

Laurie, Bob, Mike, and Brooke are all laughing hysterically.

"Your parents are potheads!" Bob declares, with that affectionate smile of his.

"I had no idea!" Brooke says, laughing that laugh where she wrinkles up her nose.

Mike: "You guys really gotta lay off the dope!"

Even with the spiral stairs, the splintered and slanted dock, the deep sand dunes, even with Henry's leg pain, we rearrange ourselves and find new possibilities for having fun.

The rest of the beach week, whenever Henry and I leave the gathering in the living room or dining room, whenever we head down the spiral staircase to go to bed, Bob or Laurie or Mike or Brooke jokes, "Uh-oh, look out! They're going off to smoke a joint!"

If one of us drops a fork or forgets a word, we hear them tease, "Those kids! They're probably high!"

Those kids. All the things we used to be. Aging foists itself on us from without. Within, we're still *those kids,* smoking a joint, acting crazy. In our minds, we can move about in time and space.

54

Henry has taught himself to drive with his left foot, tucking his right foot behind his left. He's happy to have this new freedom, this lack of limits. No more moving one digit at a time.

Today he's out running errands. I'm at my rolltop desk, the last gift my father gave me before he died. I'm enjoying my freedom, also. The sky out the window is blue. No disturbances at all.

The phone rings. I glance at Caller ID.

It's the physiatrist.

Six months since Henry last saw him in the hospital.

In a quick move, I open my drawer, pull out a yellow pad, grab a pen. I'm already picturing reporting to Henry everything this doctor has to say.

.

The following is not verbatim, but a close approximation of our conversation:

ME: Hello?
PHYSIATRIST: Mrs. Goldman? This is Dr. _____.

I'm too stunned to say anything.

PHYSIATRIST: Uh, I promised Henry I'd get back to him. I've been trying to find out stuff . . . I wanted to tell him some things I dug up. I know it's been a long recovery . . . I know it's been a terrible pain for him. I've talked to some of the doctors who've been taking care of him and . . . I know it's been a slow recovery. I've talked to Henry's doctor at the rehab facility and he's been keeping me up to date. I promised Henry I'd get information for him . . . I've been trying to look into things.

ME: When you say you promised Henry you'd get information for him, are you referring to when you saw him back in April, almost six months ago, when he was in the hospital?

This is just what I do. When I'm angry, I don't act angry. I get sarcastic.

PHYSIATRIST: Well, I've tried talking to different people, but people don't want to talk about it. They're afraid of a lawsuit. It's called "discoverable" . . . [*unsure of his exact words here*]. It's difficult. They're afraid of medical malpractice. So mostly I've been getting stuff from the Internet. How is Henry? Is he still improving or has he plateaued?

ME: Well, I don't know. It's hard to say. We really can't tell if he's still improving or if he's plateaued.

Now I'm acting like I'm simply answering a question, like I'm doing my best to report with accuracy.

PHYSIATRIST: Does he still have to wear his foot brace?
ME: Oh, yes. He can't walk without it.

My tone of voice says that anyone who has kept up with Henry would know this.

PHYSIATRIST: Well, if he's mad at me, I would understand. It's just that I promised him I would look into this. I know it's been hard for him . . . Would you have him call me? Or I'll just call him later. I don't want to intrude on you . . .
ME: Why don't you give me your number and he can call you?
PHYSIATRIST: I'll give you my home number and he can just call me at home tonight. Or any time . . . Well, maybe I'll give you my pager number because I'll probably be in transition when he calls. *He gives me a number.* If he doesn't want to talk to me, I'll understand. If he's upset with me, it won't hurt my feelings. I promised to get back to him, but it's just that there's not much information out there.
ME: I'll give him your message.
PHYSIATRIST: Thank you, Mrs. Goldman.

55

Letter received five days later:

Dear Dr. Goldman:

There are two reasons for this letter. One is to follow up on the conversation we had in the hospital after your procedure and the other is to express my deepest regrets and apologies for all you've experienced following your complications from the epidural steroid injection.

First, I am sorry I did not speak with you earlier. After you were transferred to the rehab facility, I had several conversations with your physician there. He was keeping me informed as to your condition. When he told me that you were having trouble adapting to your injury, I decided not to get in touch with you for a period of time because I didn't want to interfere with your recuperation. However, I never stopped inquiring about your progress, even after you'd left the facility and begun your outpatient rehabilitation. I do not know if keeping my distance was the right decision. The rehab doctor had suggested that 6 months after a conus injury might be a good time for a follow-up so that's when I decided to call you. When I spoke with your wife the other day, she sounded angry, and I felt I should not pursue any more contact. That's why I'm writing this letter.

Please know that I think of you constantly. I am genuinely sorry for how distressing the past months must have been for you. When a patient experiences a complication from any type of medical care, the physician always feels great sadness and guilt. I've never had any serious problem with the injections but I am now experiencing the remorse I've heard about from other physicians who have faced this type of situation. Of course, your feelings are certainly stronger than any feelings I might be having because you're the one going through this. I will not stop hoping for continued improvement for you and maybe a sense of tranquility, eventually, for both of us.

To follow up on the conversation you and I had that day in the hospital, the physicians I have spoken with believe the most likely explanation for your injury is a vascular infarction of the conus medullaris of the spinal cord. It can't be said for sure whether it was caused by the particulate matter associated with the corticosteroid or by vasospasm. I believe that the article I printed for you is still the best explanation for your situation.

Sincerely,

_____, *M.D.*

A carefully worded letter—maybe written by an attorney, maybe written by the physiatrist and then reviewed and rewritten by an attorney. We don't like the part about Henry having difficulty adapting to the injury. Wouldn't most people have difficulty adapting to paralysis? And we think that his excuse for not contacting us for six months sounds pretty flimsy. But really, nothing he states in the letter changes anything. And nothing Henry could write back or say in a phone call would change anything. So we just let it be.

56

Henry has progressed from a walker to a four-pronged cane to a regular cane. His physical therapist is now encouraging him to strengthen his leg muscles by walking in the house without his leg brace. This morning, wearing sneakers and no brace, stabbing the floor with his cane, he crosses the kitchen to the table, holding a plate with a bagel spread with cream cheese and smoked salmon, pushed to the side to make room for a mug of coffee also on the plate.

I'm at the sink, rinsing my cereal bowl.

All of a sudden, the tip of his right sneaker, that drop foot, catches on the wood floor, and he lurches forward. He tries to right himself, twisting his torso, arms flailing, cane flying, but he can't stop himself. He blunders into a fall, a dark presence moving slow motion, almost gracefully, in front of the big window, shutting off all the morning light.

Salmon, bagel, plate, mug, coffee sail through the air—white mug, tan liquid, orange fish, flowery plate, everywhere.

His face clips the sharp corner of the pine table. He lands hard on the floor.

Then a hollow silence.

"Oh my God! Are you all right?" I scream, running to him, my hands dripping dishwater.

"I *don't* think I *am* all right!" he gasps. He's holding his eye and all I can see is blood. (He still takes a blood thinner.) I can't tell where the blood is coming from, just that it's gushing. Down his neck. Darkening the gray of his T-shirt. "I think I broke my nose! I don't know whether or not I broke any of the orbital bones!"

He tells me to call the ophthalmologist whom he used to refer patients to when he was in practice. The ophthalmologist's receptionist says to come in right away.

For sure, we enjoy advantages not everyone has. Some of this has to do with Henry's being a doctor. Some of it has to do with our having lived in Charlotte for so many years and establishing long relationships with our doctors. And a lot of it has to do with the doctors themselves—their commitment and availability. When Henry and I are feeling sorry for ourselves, we need a nudge to remind us how privileged we are.

.

An X-ray shows there's no damage to the orbital bones. The ophthalmologist finds no corneal or retinal damage. He stitches Henry just above the eye, sends him to an ear, nose, and throat doctor, who confirms that Henry's nose is broken. There's nothing to be done for that.

Henry will not go without his leg brace again.

57

An old Erma Bombeck quote: "I've seen mothers fight to keep from running down the aisle at their daughter's or son's wedding, screaming, 'Wait! I'm not finished with you yet!'"

Is there a mother out there who could not list all the things she just didn't get around to teaching her children?

Henry and I were walking on the beach with Laurie and Mike (in their teens), far enough into the cool water to slosh our feet. Henry happened to use a Yiddish word. *Mittenderinnen*. Laurie and Mike had no idea what he was talking about. Henry and I looked at each other; we knew exactly what the other was thinking: *We failed to teach them Yiddish? How did that happen?*

The rest of the week was a crash course. *Meshuganah! Do you at least know that? Mishpocheh? Definitely important! Here's how you say it: Mish-puck-uh! Kvetch? You know, like someone kvetching? Complaining? Do you understand? Mensch? Schande?*

.

What else did we fail to teach?

Henry was rapturous that both Laurie and Mike inherited his athletic ability. The fact that they both turned out to be good writers dizzied my senses. They have our strengths! We can hardly tell where we end and they begin!

But our weaknesses? Which of those got divvied out?

Laurie has a temper. And she's usually late. Like Henry.

Mike is rigid in his punctuality. And assembling something from IKEA—even screwing in a light bulb—can perplex him. Like me.

Mike always left wet towels on his bedroom rug. Not like Henry or me.

Laurie got a tattoo even after we begged her not to. And then she got another one. *Who is this person?*

.

When a baby is born, anything seems possible. We see our very best selves in the making. Here comes the new-and-improved version of me! But then they grow as if driven by a restlessness. Things will live in them we never expected. We'll be overwhelmed by what we failed to teach. We'll be overwhelmed at their beautiful flowering.

58

Henry's left knee—his good leg—is hurting. Jim says it's due to the added stress on that leg. He wants him to see an orthopedist. Maybe physical therapy will help. Maybe arthroscopic surgery. Nothing major, Jim is guessing.

I go with Henry to the orthopedist. After X-rays, the doctor comes into the exam room. He's movie-star good-looking. Great haircut. Gorgeous jacket and tie. He helps Henry onto the table, examines his knee. Then he brings Henry up to a sitting position. He flashes the X-rays on the computer screen and gets down to business.

"You need a total knee replacement," he says.

"Not a partial?" I ask, before Henry can even react. "Not arthroscopic? How about physical therapy? Would acupuncture help?" *He can't have an operation. I won't let it happen.*

"No, none of those would do any good. He needs a new knee."

"Do you realize how dangerous surgery could be for my husband?"

"Mrs. Goldman," he says with a forced patience, "it's dangerous for him to try to walk with two legs that aren't working."

With that, my heart goes wild, I can scarcely breathe, I can't swallow, I'm going to faint.

"Quick, Henry! Get off the table! I have to lie down!" I hear myself saying.

Poor Henry: Knee hurting. Foot flapping. Cane banging. Wife shoving him off the table. Later we'll laugh about this. But for now, everything just feels shaky.

Henry manages to climb down from the table, hobble over to a chair. The whole room is spinning and turning blotchy—there are pieces missing from everything that crosses my line of vision. Somehow, I get myself up on the table and lie down. I think I must be as white as the paper rolled out beneath me. The surgeon checks my pulse, reaches for smelling salts, runs them under my nose.

I've never met this doctor before in my life. I'm sure he's never had a patient's spouse react this way. It's only a routine knee replacement. Most wives don't faint when surgery is recommended. Maybe he thinks I don't want my husband to get all the attention. Maybe he thinks I'm just a wacko. I can't begin to explain why the thought of Henry's surgery feels so perilous.

59

"Hey, Mom! Laurie and I would like to meet you for lunch, to strategize for Dad's surgery." It's Mike calling. "Can you do it today? Say, noon?"

Strategize? What does *strategize* mean?

Do they want to reassure me they'll be here for us? Which would not be unusual. Throughout these long months, they've each found ways to ease our lives— calling to check on their dad, picking up something we need at Costco, dropping by to move a heavy pot on the porch or fix our e-mail. Maybe they want to tell me about a plan they've worked out for who'll spend which nights in the hospital. Maybe I'll stay the first night and they'll take the others, however many there are.

I feel incapable of handling what's coming on. I don't want to ratchet up my watchfulness again. I don't want this surgery. I'm still thinking if I concentrate, if I focus, I can come up with something better than surgery.

On the other hand, maybe the kids are going to

criticize me in some way. Not that they're normally critical. They're just the opposite. But I feel so unsure of my actions these days, I imagine some sort of criticism is due. I don't think I could take it; I wouldn't trust myself to respond correctly.

Just listen to what they have to say, I tell myself. *You don't need to react. Hear them out.*

·

The three of us order salads and chat a little about Lucy and Zoe and Tess.

Mike is ready to start us off, that soft expression on his face. "Mom," he says, "Laurie and I want you to know you will not go through this alone. We'll be there whenever you need us. We'll stay with Dad as many nights as you'd like. And we'll take turns being there during the day."

Laurie goes next, her glorious energy springing across the table, as though she can infuse me with it. "Yeah, Mom, we don't want you getting exhausted while Dad's in the hospital. You're going to need your strength when he comes home. Just call on us, for anything. *Anything.*"

Oh, this is easy. I like it! Why would I have expected anything less from two loving people so skilled in empathy?

"And, Mom." Mike now. "There's one other thing." Pause.

Pause?

"We want to discuss the way you talk to the nurses and aides in the hospital. Well, actually, it's not how you talk to them. That's okay. Although your voice could be a little . . . lighter. But mostly it's . . . well, I guess it's the look on your face when you talk to them. Laurie and I understand where that expression comes from."

"It's fear," Laurie adds. "Fear that something bad will happen to Dad. We understand that."

"But to someone who doesn't know you," Mike finishes, "you just look . . . angry. You know I understand. It's hard *not* to feel angry. But you'll be more helpful to Dad if you figure out a way to curb it."

They *are* criticizing me! I can't believe it! My facial expression is the *last* thing I'm concerned about right now! Yes, I'm afraid something else will happen to their dad. And I *do* get angry when people mess up and terrible things happen. What do my kids expect? And why would they pick now to point out the things I do wrong?

I force myself to take a deep breath, to try to absorb their words.

Of course they don't like my hospital personality. It must feel pretty foreign to them. I was the permissive parent. When Laurie was applying to colleges, Henry and I grounded her for not finishing her application essays by our deadline. But then a boy she really liked asked her out for a date. "Just go," I told her. Why would we say no? I'm the parent who thought it was fine for teenage Mike to spend hours on the phone with his girlfriend. My thinking? It's important for an adolescent to be well rounded. Besides, there's nothing like young love. Henry's view? Laurie was grounded; she should stay grounded. And Mike should be doing his homework, not chatting with his girlfriend. Henry's view of me? Overindulgent. I couldn't count how many times he and I argued over disciplining the kids.

No wonder I was easy. "Don't push it" was my mother's pet expression. She wrote me excuses from school if I was tired. "You don't need to work so hard," she told me. "B's are just as good as A's."

.

Could Mike and Laurie be right? Maybe there *have* been times when I've made things worse for Henry by being so hypervigilant. I'll give my kids that. All the questioning on my part, second-guessing doctors and nurses, never letting my guard down. I've gotten riled up when I should've remained calm. And I *can* look harsh. I'm the type of person who, if I'm not smiling, just looks sad. Or mad. And my voice is normally so southern and "sweet," if I go even the least bit hardline, I can sound snippy. Not the most direct route to endearing myself to the people taking care of my husband.

What else have my children failed to teach me?

"If you stay calm." Mike is still petitioning. "If you keep yourself from getting worried and keyed up.

If you can control your fears. If you're patient with the nurses and aides—try to smile, Mom!—they'll be more willing to help."

I need to listen. Anchor myself in what they're saying. But everything feels so fragile. There's nothing to grab hold of. Besides, I'm tired.

60

One funny thing about knee-replacement surgery:

In the presurgery information packet Henry receives in the mail from the orthopedist's office is a brochure titled: *Sex After Joint Replacement.*

Regardless of whether you've replaced a shoulder, knee, or hip, there's a position just right for you. The illustrations are line drawings of old people (white hair, double chins, saggy stomachs) who are wearing bathing suits but still managing to have sex in every imaginable way. Detailed instructions included.

Under the heading "Setting the Scene," it says that having sex can be a little easier if you plan ahead. It suggests taking pain medication about twenty to thirty minutes before. *But wait. Not too much medication! Imagine how many old people fall asleep in the middle. Oh, and you should have pillows and rolled towels nearby. Also, you need to relax.*

POSITIONS (AND DESCRIPTIONS):

1. FACE-TO-FACE: Being on the bottom is safe for a man or a woman with a new joint. Use pillows or rolled towels to support

the legs on the outside. Depending on comfort, the person on the bottom can recline propped up on pillows, or lie flat.

2.   SITTING IN A CHAIR: The man sits on a straight chair. His feet are supported or are flat on the floor. The woman sits on the man's lap.

3.   WOMAN LYING AND MAN KNEELING: The woman lies on the bed on her back, hips near the edge of the bed. Both feet should be supported or flat on the floor. The man kneels in front of the woman, on pillows placed on the floor. [*I'm thinking it must be a very low bed.*]

4.   SIDE-LYING POSITION: This position works for a man with a replaced knee joint. He should lie on his side, with the new joint on the bottom. Use pillows for support. [*But where is the woman?*]

All those bubbly old people, with their brand-new body parts, going at it.

61

A year and eight months after the epidural, Henry has knee-replacement surgery. Afterward, the orthopedic surgeon meets with Laurie, Mike, and me in a little side room. He's the movie-star-handsome doc who had to use smelling salts on me. I'll bet he has really been looking forward to operating on my husband so that he can encounter me again! It suddenly occurs to me who he looks like: George Clooney, in green scrubs and those slippers that look like paper shower caps. There's a broad smile on his face. *Good. Henry's okay.*

But then he tells us he was surprised to find so much nerve damage in the leg he operated on, the "good" leg. He's had to place that leg in a stabilizer, which will stay on for three days. Normally, he explains, knee-replacement patients are up walking immediately, to promote healing. But Henry will have to stay in bed. Can't risk a fall.

Here we go. That click in my head. *What else did we not anticipate?*

.

Over Henry's objections, I decide to spend the night in his room. Laurie and Mike offer to stay, but I tell them I'd rather be with him the first night. An aide sets up a cot next to the bed, with pillow, sheets, and blanket. I kiss Henry good night, switch off the lights, we settle in. He goes right to sleep, his quiet snores like soft chimes.

Around ten, a nurse comes in to check his vital signs. Blood pressure low.

Not sure how much time goes by, but it seems as though she just left when she returns. I hear an accent when she speaks. I can't make out her features in the dark, but I can tell she's tiny. I ask where she's from. A small coastal town in the Philippines. We chat a little about that, and then I work in my question: How's his blood pressure now? Low, she says. She turns the monitor so I can see. Dangerously low. "He must have lost so much blood during surgery," she says, "he could be going into shock."

I feel the labor in my breath. I lift my head, raise up on my elbow, look at her petite silhouette, glance over at Henry, still sleeping. He's turned away from me. I see the back of his head, his hair a mess, the worn, pebbly hospital blanket tucked around his neck. I want to scoop him up, take him home, get him well. But what I do is lie back down in silence.

The nurse leaves quickly and returns quickly, wheeling in a machine that—from what I can understand from her explanation—will remove his blood, do something to it, then run it back through his body. A blood transfusion using your own blood. Sort of a recycling. I'm too fuzzy with the beginnings of sleep to really understand. I see, though, that she doesn't leave the room. She just stands there, in the dark, at the foot of his bed, monitoring the machine that's carrying on its mysterious work. I'm on my back, the sheet and blanket up to my shoulders. I can see the blood pressure numbers from my cot. I do not look away, even for a second. I make myself become something firm and closed off, so I can concentrate. Bring the numbers up.

And if I'm friendly to the nurse, I can report back to Laurie and Mike that I took their advice.

I make an effort to relax, and I joke, "You know, this feels like we're on a reality TV show, my husband and me in bed, you watching!" She and I laugh. If Henry were awake, he'd laugh, too.

His blood pressure is not moving.

Finally, I get up the courage to ask about consulting a doctor. She's so conscientious, so concerned, I don't want my hospital personality to ooze out. She says, in a kind voice, she has already called a doctor and these are his orders.

More hours pass. I stay focused on the numbers. I'm wide awake, but I don't move. I'm working hard. His blood pressure is still alarmingly low.

"Would you mind calling the doctor again?" I ask.

"Well, let's give it a while longer."

I force myself to try to understand. She's already

called the doctor. How would a doctor react to two phone calls in the middle of the night about the same patient? It makes sense, her response. *See, Laurie and Mike? See how I listen?*

I start sending my prayers directly into the machine, *Please, go up. Go up! Go up!*

Finally, morning coming on, the numbers change direction. By the time the carts carrying breakfast trays clank down the hall, he's out of danger.

When it's time for a shift change and our nurse comes in to say good-bye, she and I hug. I wish I had a small, wrapped gift for her. At the very least, home-made muffins. A potted fern.

.

The next morning, a new problem: fever.

Our new nurse asks, "Has your husband been using the incentive spirometer?"

"What's an incentive spirometer?" I say.

Apparently, it's an apparatus a patient should use regularly after surgery to keep the lungs clear. Unfortunately, Henry was not given one. Now he has pneumonia.

If Laurie and Mike were observing me now, they would not approve of the way my mouth is drawn to one side, a look that says this nurse is to blame for purposely withholding the incentive spirometer from Henry—a look that doesn't take into consideration it could have been the doctor who forgot to order it, or an aide who had it on her cart but delivered it to the wrong room, or that it got delivered to Henry's room but somebody accidentally knocked it off the table into the trash. It's a look that says I'm not letting down my guard for a minute. It's a look that says I don't care how I look.

62

We were getting dressed to go to our neighbors' for dinner. They'd invited friends and family over to celebrate their son's graduation from high school. It was early June. *Prairie Home Companion* was on the radio in our bedroom, an accordion playing a rowdy old song. Our windows were open, tree branches blowing back and forth outside. Henry had pulled out a short-sleeved knit polo shirt to wear. It was one I liked, a pale green. But I didn't think it was appropriate for a dinner party.

"Shouldn't you wear a button-down?" I asked, acting as though I was asking a question he could answer any way he liked.

"No. I don't think it's necessary. This is fine." Wrong answer.

He was sitting on his side of the bed, arms raised, letting the shirt fall over his head. He already had on his khakis. I was wearing a white silk blouse and beige pants. I was even wearing earrings. I sat backward on my dressing-table bench, looking in my little hand mirror, combing the back of my hair.

"You know," I said, "I'm thinking the other men there will probably be more dressed up. Don't you think a button-down would be better?"

He inched his way back out of the polo shirt, placed it on the bed, and crossed the room to his closet. This wasn't done with any type of attitude. In fact, he had a sweet smile on his face.

I heard him in the closet, shifting coat hangers. He emerged holding his dark blue checked button-down. Exactly what I thought he should wear. Perfect with his khaki pants. Perfect for the occasion.

"See how I listen to you?" he said, laughing.

"See how you like to point it out?" I said, laughing.

I love when we make everything sound like a joke.

As it turned out, he was the only male at the party not wearing a polo shirt. He never mentioned it. Another thing I dearly love.

63

No one really knows what goes on inside somebody else's marriage, except for the people who are in it. Still, we look at the marriages around us and draw conclusions. We even wonder about our children's marriages. And we often have opinions.

Do I tell them my opinions? Sometimes. (Not a good idea.)

Should I put my opinions in a book? (A really bad idea.)

But this book is about marriage, about why and how two people come together and why and how they stay together, so part of what I think about marriage includes what I think about my children's marriages. Just as Henry and I have done (are doing), our children and their spouses are figuring out a way to shape a long-term marriage. All that robust effort, recovery and rebuilding.

Of course, this chapter could be viewed by my kids as a giant overstepping. So I sent it to them to see if they had a problem with anything I'd written. They didn't.

First, Laurie and Bob:

They bond through humor—what's funny to her is funny to him. They have a thousand private jokes, which—no matter how often the same one pops up—seem to not only bring them laughter, but contentment. I see them bonding through a shared consciousness about the world and its unjustness and how they can make it more just. They believe in the complete rightness of things, in honest possibilities. They're empathetic, kind. But. Laurie is an extrovert. Bob is an introvert. Laurie needs to talk about every little thing happening in her life, her observations, what she knows, what sucks her down or lifts her. He smiles, reads, cleans up after dinner, disappears into the next room, takes a solitary hike up Crowder Mountain. She can get mad. Really mad. When she was a teenager, she kicked in a closet door. Bob does not appear to get mad. He gets quiet.

How are they as parents? Both are affectionate, both involved. Laurie is the same kind of mother I was, the same as *my* mother. Loving. Bob is loving, too, but stricter—I suspect it's the way his father, a state trooper, probably was. So when Lucy or Zoe gets off-kilter, I see Laurie touch Bob's arm as if she's marking it clearly: *I'll handle this, you can back off, this is a time for looseness.* And I've seen Bob insist that Lucy and Zoe take their plates into the kitchen after dinner, scrape them and put them in the dishwasher, even while Laurie is shaking her head no, no, not necessary, just go play.

I don't know how often Laurie gets her way. Don't know how often Bob gets his.

.

And Mike and Brooke?

I see them holding hands under the dinner table, kissing as Brooke brushes past Mike on her way out of the room. Sometimes they look at each other as though the rest of the world has vanished. A lovely open affection between them. Both Mike and Brooke have a bone-deep intuition about the natural order of things. A psychological savvy. Mike comes home with a dilemma from work, and the two of them deconstruct it, then construct a solution. Also, what I see, over and over, is their perseverance to aim for and achieve goals. The two of them get things done. Brooke has a sureness about her. A strong certainty. And now Mike has that same certainty. The way one spouse rubs off on another. Oh, and I wish you could see them dance!

They, like Laurie and Bob, are loving, involved parents. Brooke is out there in the backyard throwing the football with Benjamin. Mike coaches Tess's basketball team.

I also see Mike and Brooke exchanging words about their kids' bedtimes.

"They need to go to bed. You know how grouchy they are when they don't get their sleep." That's Brooke.

"They can stay up a little longer. It won't hurt them." Mike.

I'm usually on the it's-a-special-occasion side, which means we push back bedtime for the children—especially in summer, when dark's so late. Really, I can build a case for letting kids stay up in any season. At the same time, I remember the beach trip when Benjamin was allowed to stay up way past his bedtime. The next day, he was so tired he just cried all day long. I have a video on my phone of him laughing at something funny, laughing, laughing, and then the laughter suddenly breaking down into sobs.

I don't know how often Mike gets his way. Don't know how often Brooke gets hers.

·

There are times I really like what I see and hear in my children's marriages. And times when I don't. Sort of like my own marriage.

64

Since The Accident (is that what we call it?), various physicians—friends of ours, as well as docs Henry sees professionally—have asked us to explain to them what happened. The truth is, we don't really know. So here are their questions. Without any answers.

1. A neurosurgeon (an acquaintance of ours) wondered if the numbness after the first epidural should have been a red flag, if that level of numbness could have been indicative of a problem that might preclude a second epidural.
2. A neurosurgeon and an anesthesiologist, both acquaintances of ours, questioned why the physiatrist did not withdraw the needle at Henry's first mention of pain.
3. The anesthesiologist for Henry's knee-replacement surgery expressed surprise that he'd been given an epidural for spinal stenosis after the stenosis had been surgically repaired. The anesthesiologist said that the space could be awfully narrow for an injection, that he would not have administered

that epidural. "Nor would any of my twenty-five partners," he added.

4. Doctors have mentioned the small window of opportunity during which a medical complication might be neutralized. Was there a window of opportunity for Henry? Did we miss it? Could the physiatrist have reversed the paralysis resulting from the epidural if he had been more interested in trying to find out what went wrong than in telling us how many injections he'd safely given?

5. Doctors have asked us if we know whether the physiatrist was referring to the volume of the formula or the concentration when he told us he gave Henry the "Saddam shot, the mother of all shots." The answer could point the way to the cause of paralysis.

65

So we come to the question: Should we sue?

Until now, we've been too busy trying to impose order on chaos. But now, two years after the epidural, Henry and I are discussing the possibility of consulting an attorney.

Henry's condition, at this point:

He walks with a cane, tires easily. Cannot raise or lower his right foot. Wears a brace on that leg to offset the foot drop. Neuropathy in both feet, worse in right. Poor balance. Prone to infection in both legs, both feet. Repeated blood clots. Repeated gout. Pain in right hip and calf. Night spasms in "good," left leg. Frequent and urgent urination (neurogenic bladder). On antidepressant. Must continue physical therapy indefinitely.

·

Henry and I find ourselves falling into some sort of gravitational pull: He definitely wants to pursue legal action; I say why would we want to put ourselves through more anguish? Then we switch. I say we should at least check into litigation; he says he doesn't think it's worth it. Back and forth. We're wearing ourselves down. We have family meetings with Laurie and Bob and Mike and Brooke. They weigh the pros and cons with us but, in the end, insist it's our decision. Even if Henry and I *could* make up our minds, there doesn't seem to be enough time for us to take the first step. We just can't find a space wide enough to pick through.

·

But here we are, Henry, Mike, and I, seated across the desk from a Charlotte lawyer who is well respected for his work in medical malpractice. He's slim, has a longish face and a well-groomed beard. His manner is understated, competent, courteous. He asks questions. One of us supplies an answer; sometimes two of us talk at once, sometimes all three of us. A few of his questions stump us, and there's only silence from our side of the desk. Mostly, there are more than enough pieces of information to provide. All these particulars floating in the air above us.

·

I kept extensive notes, beginning hours after the epidural, throughout Henry's recuperation. Not because I thought of suing. I was doing what I'd always done: writing to make sense of something that did not make sense. Maybe I was trying to regain a sense of control over the ever-changing world we found ourselves in. As I began writing this chapter for my memoir, though, I realized I did not take notes on our meeting with the lawyer. And I don't want to use vague recollection as background. My memories of the first meeting, and subsequent meetings, with this attorney are blurry. I do remember handing him a list of the large and small consequences Henry deals with as a result of the injection. I remember reading the list aloud as he followed along on the paper.

Picture Henry, Mike, and me in the meeting, across from the attorney, whom Henry and I have known slightly for years. I swallow hard before I read aloud the part about Henry's not being able to engage in intercourse as a result of nerve damage. I can't look at the attorney's face. I can't look at our son's face. I bear down on that paper, my voice rising and falling.

At this point, I don't know that this problem will happily resolve in time.

I also don't know yet that this attorney will spend the better part of a year pursuing our case. He'll search the records, consult medical experts, call us with follow-up questions. But in the end, he'll give us a very compassionate, yet firm, no. We don't have a case.

Of course, we knew all along how difficult it would be to prove negligence. Our attorney, along with a medical expert, had to address the two questions central to any medical malpractice case: Did the doctor follow the standard of care for doctors in the same situation? Did the doctor's failure to follow the standard of care injure Henry?

After our lawyer calls with his final decision, Henry looks at me and utters an expression his mother used to say: "It's *bashert*." Which means *meant to be*. A Yiddish *Que sera sera*. *Bashert* can refer to any chance event whose consequences might at first appear negative but ultimately turn out positive. ("I missed the bus, but it must have been *bashert*, because I heard it broke down.")

Months later, though, Henry runs into a guy he used to know back when he played racquetball at the Y. When he hears all that has happened, he strongly recommends that Henry see his friend, an attorney here in town who handles medical malpractice. This pitches us right back into the same vacillation. Should we sue? Should we just let go? We end up meeting with the attorney. At this point, it almost feels like an afterthought. Still, we hand over the medical notes I kept during the past two years, go home, and wait to hear if he thinks we have a case.

66

Letter from that second attorney:

Dear Dr. Goldman:

You have requested that we review whether you can bring a claim for medical malpractice. In doing so, we have looked at several preliminary issues which bear on your right to bring such a claim and our ability to represent you in such a claim.

First, a medical malpractice claim is considered to be a claim for negligence. In North Carolina, the statute of limitations to bring such a claim is generally three years from the date of injury. This means that you have a deadline of three years from that date to file your claim against the healthcare provider. After that, you forfeit your right to recover damages from any malpractice.

Second, you must be able to show that the medical provider breached the applicable standard of care. The standard of care is the proper approach, practice, or procedure for a particular medical situation that is accepted by the medical community in a particular geographic location. If the provider did not meet the standard of care, then there is negligence.

Third, you must be able to prove that you suffered injuries that were proximately caused by the breach of the standard of care. That is to say, you must be able to prove that your injuries resulted from or were because of a breach of the standard of care.

Proof of the second and third issues requires that a qualified medical expert review the medical records prior to filing a claim and be willing to testify that the standard of care was not met and that injury resulted.

Finally, you must be able to prove—with expert testimony—the extent of damages to which you are entitled. Medical malpractice cases are typically expert-driven and thus can be very costly. Expert testimony is expensive and we would need to pay not only the costs of the expert's time, but also any expenses, including travel. It would not be unusual to spend anywhere up to $80,000 before you even get to the trial of your case.

We have examined all of these issues in connection with your matter and determined that we are not in a position to represent you. This doesn't mean that your case is without merit as our opinion about your case and decisions about representation may differ from other attorneys.

If you decide to seek an additional opinion, however, we strongly urge you to do so quickly given the statute of limitations noted above.

Sincerely,

Lawyer Unable to Take the Case

One year after knee replacement, two years after the epidural, Henry needs a total shoulder replacement. Again, his altered gait and awkward posture have created problems in other body parts. Again, my heart goes tight as a blister. *No. He's not going to have this surgery. Definitely not. You're wrong. That's not what he needs. Let's think. Focus. Together we can come up with a better plan.*

But he does have the surgery. And all goes well. During his days in the hospital, there are junctures when things could go awry, but the orthopedist stays very involved and every nurse who could make a difference *does* make a difference. Each threat is bypassed.

Smooth hospital stay. Followed by smooth recovery.

"The dry cleaning's in the backseat," Henry says. "Let's swing by and drop it off, since we're close." It's too soon after Henry's shoulder surgery for him to get behind the wheel, so I'm driving. I roll down my window. It's one of those warm afternoons in December that North Carolina is famous for. Clear and cloudless.

I drive through the parking lot of the dry cleaner, up to the pinkish stucco building, ease in as close as I can to what used to be a drive-by window but is now a drive-by door. I do a great job of getting close without scraping, twist around for Henry's khakis and my sweater, thinking I'll hand them over, through my open window. But I can't reach the clothes. To help me maneuver, Henry takes my handbag from my lap. I turn off the engine, put the car in park, pull up the emergency brake, get out, scoop up the pants and sweater.

By this time, the owner, a small, middle-aged Asian man, has opened the drive-by door and is standing in the threshold. I shut my rear door. The driver's side is still open.

I'm about to place the clothes in his arms when a stringy young man bolts from inside the dry cleaner and pushes right between the owner and me. The three of us are now wedged in this tiny space. To anyone driving past, we must look like an intimate little gathering. We're so close we could hug, or brush dandruff off one another's shoulders.

My first thought: *Oh, this guy works here. He's rushing out to take over for his boss.* I glance up. *But why is he wearing a ski cap?*

My second thought: *It's not a ski cap.*

It's a ski mask.

Which reveals only his eyes.

Focused on me.

My eyes move down his body to his hand. He's holding a pistol. Aimed at my abdomen. His finger on the trigger.

From where Henry is sitting, he can't see a thing. Whatever I decide to do next will be just that: my decision. Totally up to me.

I sling the clothes across the driver's seat into Henry's lap, jump back into the car, grab the handle, slam my heavy door shut. All in one swift motion.

My window is still down. The guy could easily shoot me through the opening. He's six inches away. If he wanted, he could reach in and grab my neck.

I turn the key, let off the brake, put the car in gear. My arms and legs feel leaden. But I push myself with everything I have, push to move faster, faster, saying out loud, over and over, in a voice my harsh breathing makes throaty: "Quick! Quick! Quick!"

Then I speed away.

"Call the police!" I yell, my whole mind willing Henry to hurry. By this time, he knows what's happening. "Reach in my handbag! Get my cell phone! It's already on!"

But Henry, way too slowly—you will never see my husband rush, not ever—leans over on one hip, reaches into his pants pocket for *his* phone, a motion made awkward by his new shoulder, his seat belt, my handbag, and the dry cleaning in his lap. Now he's flipping his phone open, punching the button to turn it on. I hear the familiar chimes. Then he slowly and painstakingly hits those three numbers, a turtle's pace: 911. *Why wouldn't he just use my phone?*

When we get home, he calls the dry cleaner. The owner is okay. He tells Henry the police did arrive, but too late. The guy had already taken all his cash.

·

For days afterward, I find myself crying. I can be washing my hair or fastening my bra or meeting a friend to walk in the neighborhood, and my eyes will suddenly well with tears.

I keep seeing the gun. The sleek shape of it. The steely shade of charcoal gray. I can almost smell its hot breath.

I see the ski mask. How incongruous it seemed at

first for a face to be covered in black wool when it was sixty-five degrees out.

I replay everything with Henry. He listens. I replay. I cry. He pats my hand. I cry.

Sad. That's the emotion I feel. Why sad? Frightened, haunted, even angry over what happened to the owner of the dry cleaner—sure. But *sad*?

Just when things are going well with Henry and me, this despair? It does not make sense. I should feel grateful for Henry's good health, grateful we weren't hurt in the holdup. Really, no big deal.

But it all feels so personal. Clammy. Punishing. As though this small, insignificant incident has a wide reach. Everything suddenly laid open. A hammer has been brought down, smashing off an irregular piece of my head and sending it flying.

·

I find myself telling the story of the holdup over and over. I want everyone to know. At a dinner party, I make my friends join me in a reenactment.

"Okay, John, you be the owner of the dry cleaner. And you, Bobbie, be the robber. Just jump out, Bobbie. Like this. And hold your gun lower. Point it at my stomach. Wait, both of you stand here. No, closer." I pull the two of them right up to me. We're huddled together. "Yeah," I say, "that's it." I'm making it funny so that we can all laugh—my fellow actors *and* our audience.

I go home from the dinner and cry.

•

Time passes. All of a sudden, I get it. Because somebody threatened me with a gun, I can finally cry—*really cry*—over what threatened Henry in that outpatient clinic two years ago. As though the holdup and the epidural are one thing. One single reminder that we're all in danger every second. The world is waiting to trip us up. Our lives can change when we make a quick decision to try some procedure that might relieve a hurting back. Our lives can end when we drop off clothes at the dry cleaner the last afternoon in December that's warm and cloudless.

69

Six months after the holdup, Dannye and Lew invite
Henry and me, along with other friends, Bobbie and
George, Laurie and John, to Highlands, North Carolina, for a long weekend in one of those old mountain
houses with knotty-pine walls. Years ago, Dannye,
book editor of *The Charlotte Observer,* had driven up
to Highlands to interview Walker Percy. She fell in
love with the house he and his wife were renting, and
she and Lew have rented it themselves every summer
since then.

They offer Henry and me the master bedroom. It's
on the main level and is the only bedroom with its
own bathroom. A very generous gesture, but we say
no, no, we couldn't, and they say yes, yes, they insist.

For four days, the eight of us tell stories, laugh,
talk politics, cook together in the kitchen, and eat
bountiful meals in captain's chairs pulled around the
dining room table.

Every morning we hike. Henry assures me he
doesn't mind my leaving him. He says that reading
on the porch, overlooking a lake with leafy branches

and ragged rocks, is fine with him. So I go. And constantly check my watch, wondering if I'm doing the right thing, or an insensitive thing.

At lunch the last day—tunafish sandwiches with Dannye's mother's recipe for potato salad, real onion juice the secret ingredient—someone mentions the hikes, how sorry they are that Henry can't join us, which leads to a conversation about his physical limitations, how they have changed him, us, his image of himself, our roles.

Suddenly, Henry and I find ourselves recounting the entire story of the Medical Mishap. We go through the whole chronology, plunging further and further, as though we have a hunger that can be satisfied only by digging deep and bringing every last detail to light. We interrupt each other with specifics the other forgets. I'm amazed at the gaps in Henry's recall, how many incidents he has no memory of. But we both talk. It feels like we're in the middle of a tumble and there's no way to stop. We've never told the story to friends, in sequence, in its entirety. Everyone sitting at this table is bighearted and indulgent and asks questions, then follow-up questions.

Which leads to: What is the role of blame here?

I wish I could say we've totally forgiven the physiatrist. Both Henry and I so want to extend the margins of our generosity, our compassion. But that's not easy for us. Each of us does have small, fleeting moments in which we forgive—sometimes both of us at the same time, sometimes only Henry, sometimes me.

Of course, we know the physiatrist didn't set out to harm Henry.

He wanted to help him.

Regardless of what went wrong with the injection, the physiatrist really doesn't deserve our censure. The mishap was—a mishap. An accident. Bad luck. Maybe an error *was* made. By the doctor. Or one of the nurses. But vilifying someone (even if only in our minds) isn't fair. If a plumber comes to the house to fix a leaky toilet and all of a sudden water floods the bathroom and the tile floor buckles and has to be replaced, we don't harbor great bitterness toward him. Whether it's a floor or a body, things can get botched. We all do the best we can.

And yet. There've been times I have felt such intense resentment toward that physiatrist I wouldn't trust myself if he walked into the room. I could not be responsible for the words I might see traveling from my mouth into the air.

What do I want from him?

Of course, there's no way he can compensate Henry for his loss.

So, what would I wish for?

An apology?

His letter was sort of an apology. Well, not really an apology. More of an explanation of why he'd been so silent.

Here's what I would've liked: An explanation of what went wrong *early on*. When it happened. And I would have liked concern. Was there anything, those first few hours, anything at all that could have been done to alter the course? I also would've liked concern ongoing. There were so many months he could have let us know he cared.

Highest on my list: He could have let us know he was doing everything he could to prevent this from happening to future patients. This would have not only benefitted others; it would have demonstrated to us in the strongest way possible that what happened to Henry was considered so important it warranted an investigation and a reordering. Instead, his focus was on himself. And those seven thousand shots he'd safely given.

70

Henry's legs have been growing weaker, both of them. The surgeon (Henry's same one from the spinal stenosis surgery) wants to run tests.

My not-surprising vote: Leave well enough alone. No invasive testing, please.

Henry's not-surprising decision: He wants the tests.

Diagnosis: more spinal stenosis. Our beloved surgeon says, "Henry, you have a horrific spine." If left untreated, he warns, this particular stenosis could cause even more paralysis. He believes surgery might also produce the added benefit of strengthening Henry's legs.

My not-surprising vote: Please, no surgery.

Henry has the surgery. No complications. In fact, the surgeon and his PA are so careful, so thorough in their follow-up, the entire episode goes smoothly.

The not-so-good news: Surgery did not strengthen Henry's legs. In fact, they're weaker. Probably Henry's horrific spine.

For his final checkup after the surgery, he goes to the appointment alone. Five years have passed since the epidural; the statute of limitations has run out; maybe the surgeon will feel free to talk. Henry asks him, "Was my case ever discussed among you and your partners?"

"Ohhh, yes," he answers, as though he's really saying, *You don't know the half of it.* And then he goes on to say something like: "Your case was discussed and discussed. In depth. In fact, physicians all over Charlotte were very interested in what happened to you."

"Did anyone ever decide what caused the problem?" Henry asks. May as well go for the whole thing, he's thinking.

His answer, as far as Henry remembers: "It was finally determined that the cause must have been chemical. The formulation. As a result, the formula in epidurals has been changed. Now, doctors in our practice—and probably doctors all over Charlotte— use a more diluted formula, less viscous. To put it in layman's terms, the liquid used to be milky in appearance. Now it's clearer. Much quicker. So it won't deliver a bolus that could interrupt the blood flow."

At the end of their conversation, the physiatrist's name is mentioned. The surgeon adds something like "He was very, *very* upset over what happened to you."

So it seems it was the formula that caused the paralysis? This is the first explanation we've been given. We have no way of judging whether this is a full, a partial, or even a wrong explanation.

Of course, Henry and I have great respect and affection for this surgeon. And we appreciate his willingness to address the subject. He certainly didn't hesitate when Henry brought it up.

But. If there *was* something wrong with the formula injected into my husband's spine, why weren't we told? Something so wrong that the formula had to be changed? Not just by the doctors in this practice. But by doctors all over Charlotte. How many Charlotte doctors changed formulas? Five? Ten? Dozens? *And nobody told us?* All those doctors, practicing in multiple locations around this city, somehow found out that the formula in my husband's hypodermic needle was too viscous? Too milky?

Milk, the pearly liquid that sustains our infants—but wait! Too much milky substance could paralyze you. Why were we left out of the loop? And when was the decision made to change the formula? Was it when Henry was stuffed into that small, hot room in the rehab facility? Was it when I was trying to get him a physical therapist for those crucial first three weeks after the injection? Was it during one of his surgeries?

That word. *Bolus.* Sounds like bowling. A game in which things that are standing get knocked down.

People say they're knocked off their pins when they're suddenly floored by a shocking turn of events. *Bolus.* I think I remember the vet prescribing a pill called a bolus for our dog, Dudley. This news *is* a large pill. A tough pill to swallow. But if we carp, if we whine, then *we're* being pills. Henry and I are so afraid of stepping into that narrowing noose of self-pity. And we don't want epic anger to run our lives. Not only is it unhealthy for us, it's—well, unattractive. Most of us avoid people who are constantly ranting.

·

Over and over, at great length, Henry and I discuss his conversation with the surgeon. It's hard, so hard, to know what to make of it. It's entirely possible we now know what happened. Certainly, this explanation lets the physiatrist off the hook. If it was the formula that all doctors were using at the time and somehow it didn't work well with Henry, then the accident is nobody's fault. No error was made. The doctor was just following the standard of care. But is there more to the story? Is this even the real story? Will we ever know for sure?

71

Henry and I were sharing an order of moo shu pork at Baoding restaurant, and I was bringing up the subject of funerals again. We were in our early seventies.

I named the two options—which we'd discussed before but could never decide between—as I smeared my pancake with hoisin sauce, filled it with crispy pork, rolled the whole thing up: Should we be cremated? Or buried?

Having been raised in an Orthodox home, Henry was unsure about cremation. Jewish law has always been unequivocal that the dead must be buried in the earth. But I knew that more and more Jews were choosing cremation. Of course, I understood his uncertainty. But I had my own uncertainties about a traditional burial—namely, the formalities and expense. Were they really necessary?

This wasn't the only end-of-life decision we weren't able to make. Since we had not belonged to a synagogue for years, we didn't know where our funerals should be held. In a funeral home? One good thing, I said, Harry & Bryant is right in the neighborhood, two blocks away, across from Ben & Jerry's. Or maybe it could be in our home. If he were healthy and energetic, or if I were, that might be a possibility. Or Laurie or Mike could host. I was asking the questions, coming up with answers. Henry was mainly eating.

And who would officiate? Would there be religious aspects to the service? I like Psalm 23, I said. Perfect for a Jewish service. I also like "Amazing Grace." Not quite right for a Jewish service.

When we got home from Baoding, I called Laurie, then Mike, and asked if they had strong opinions about what to do with our dead bodies. After my initial attempt at humor, which came off pretty well—*dead bodies* will always get a laugh—I explained the options. Each one responded exactly the way I knew they would: "It's up to you and Dad, Mom." Practical Mike added, "I *would* like y'all to decide sooner rather than later. You're not getting any younger, you know. How about if I give you a deadline? What if you tell us what you want when we're all at the beach?"

Our annual beach trip was two months away. We had a lot of talking to do.

·

One sunshiny day, not long after Baoding, on our way to buy a new mattress, we were driving from the Original Mattress Factory on Park Road to Dilworth Mattress Company in South End. It would be at least ten minutes before we could get from point A to point B, maybe longer, since it had been years since we'd been to Dilworth Mattress and we weren't exactly sure where it was.

I introduced the topic again. "I don't like being the only one constantly bringing this up. I want you to care about it as much as I do."

"Care about what?"

"Our funerals."

"Okay. Well. What do you want to do?" he said. He was taking an odd route, cutting through neighborhoods I didn't know. But he'd always been much better at directions than me. I used to joke he even knows east from west.

"It's not really what *I* want to do," I said. "It's what *we* want to do. If you think you'd rather be buried, then I want to be buried beside you. If you think it's okay to be cremated, then let's both be cremated."

"But what would we do with our ashes?"

"Well, it wouldn't be up to us," I said.

"So, then, what would our children do with our ashes?"

"They could scatter them in the ocean." This had just occurred to me, but I said it as though I'd been thinking about it for decades. "You know how we all like the beach."

"True."

What's true is that every time we had this discussion, we reached a point where it felt to both of us we'd gone as far we could go. Henry wasn't the only one not in love with the topic.

"Well, I have an idea," I said. "How about if we ask

Laurie or Mike to read 'Holding Back Winter' at each of our funerals, regardless whether we're cremated or buried, regardless where the service is held?"

"Holding Back Winter" is a poem I wrote in the 1980s, way before I understood anything about aging or death or the longing to go back in time.

HOLDING BACK WINTER

Blame it on the ginkgo leaves,
those October coins
tossed like rings or kisses
all around us.
We did not need the sun.
My face bright, a morning wish,
as I posed for your picture,
my hair browner than the bark
you caught behind me.

This very minute
I would press myself flat,
pull us both
into the snapshot
like film run backwards
drawing people back
where they once were.

There. Now we both
lean against the fence,
lean into the camera,

our eyes wide
as small suns.

How the yellow light
holds back winter,
freezes autumn
as if it were a young couple
just starting out,
before they can learn
the crusted winds
that sweep one life into the next.
That young married couple
smiling their hearts out
for a souvenir.

72

A friend, who's at least twenty years younger and divorced, asks me if there was ever a point when Henry and I might have divorced. "You know, a time you thought your trajectory would change?" Her voice is earnest. "I was really mad at the Gores when they broke up. You and Henry are like Tipper and Al. Who could ever imagine you two splitting?"

How can I explain that the most difficulty we've ever had getting along, the *only* time we've actually struggled to stay happy with each other, is now, in our seventies?

After Mike left for college and Laurie for grad school, it struck Henry and me that we were no longer arguing. We hadn't realized that the cause of most of our fights up until then had been our children. Our adolescent children. With the rooms of our house filled with two young people trying out new identities, struggling to explain the unexplainable, everything about their young lives unsettled—who Henry was as a parent and who I was as a parent got put to the test. He and I had been raised so differently. I was sure my parents were right; I was sure his parents were not right. Interestingly, he felt the same way: He admired my parents and wanted to be like them. But inlaid patterns are not easy to break apart. When the two of us were in that murky place of figuring out how to discipline teenagers, he sometimes reverted back to the rigidity of his mother. And in that way husbands and wives polarize each other, one reacting to the other, each going for the extreme, I became an exaggerated version of my mother. Way too permissive.

Both of us engaged in some sort of primitive thing.

Even at our worst, though, when we were like two mules kicking, we caught ourselves loving the other beyond all reason.

·

Why I think marriage is difficult for us now:

Once again, the rooms of our house are filled with people trying out new identities, struggling to explain the unexplainable, everything about our lives unsettled. Who Henry is, who I am—both up for grabs.

Confession: I can be cranky. When I see him at breakfast, swallowing twelve pills and vitamins all at once with one gulp of orange juice, I cringe. But cringing is not all I do. I follow up cringing with nagging. "You shouldn't swallow all those meds with so little liquid. Think what you're doing to your esophagus. You know your sister burned her esophagus doing that. You should make at least three separate piles of pills . . ." The next morning, I see him dividing the pills into two piles. Which means he's not completely opposed to what I'm saying, but the esophageal damage will be worth it if he doesn't have to cave in to me completely.

Oh, I used to be a good wife. I could have won *prizes,* I was such a good wife. A giant of patience and understanding. But there won't be any prizes now. My record is tarnished.

Why am I so cranky?

One theory: My pissiness is a way of separating myself from him. As though I'm practicing aloneness. A dress rehearsal. Although there is no way to ever rehearse death.

Another theory: I'm not only terrified I'll lose him. I'm terrified *we'll* lose *me.* Five years after Henry's epidural, I was hospitalized for pneumonia. When he took me to the ER at two in the morning, my temperature was 104, my white blood cell count sky-high. Something inside me had been pulled from its course. I was huffing through my open mouth for breaths. As the transporter wheeled me from the ER to a room, I could hear Henry, with his cane, galump-galump-galumping behind us. Then I didn't hear the galumps. "Would you just check over your shoulder every now and then," I asked the transporter, "to be sure my husband is still with us?" Henry was right there with me, though, throughout. Every day, all day, he was there. The first time Laurie came, she said, "Mom, you wouldn't believe how far it is from the parking deck to your room! How in the world is Dad doing this?"

After I got better, my doctor told me, "We nearly lost you." Those words haunted me for weeks. I can't get sick like that again. I have to stay healthy. And strong.

Which makes me even crankier. It's not fair for me to have all this responsibility. If I get sick and conk out, I want the luxury of being able to conk completely out. (Did Henry ever feel the same frustration—when he was the one we both depended on?)

.

Maybe I'm really just angry with Henry for threatening to fail physically. For even obliquely threatening to die. As though he has to earn my forgiveness for what happened to him. As though his medical condition is a betrayal. He was supposed to be the strong one. I counted on that. Was it all just a bait and switch? He won me over with his robustness. *Good. She's mine. Now I can just crumple.*

.

Oh, he can be cranky, too.

He's at the kitchen sink rinsing the dinner dishes. I'm next to him, taking each plate, glass, and fork and fitting them into the dishwasher. I place a glass in the top rack, near the front. He reaches over, takes the glass I just put in, moves it to the back. "You should load it this way," he instructs, more than a little astringency in his voice.

Why is he cranky?

Because he's tired of hobbling around on a leg that doesn't work. Tired of medical emergencies.

Tired of relying on me.

Tired of this role reversal, ready to switch back. I'm ready, too. But neither of us can figure out how to reverse a reversal.

73

Why take on the task of writing a memoir? What's the point of carrying around all those memories (grim details, bad feelings), then spending years unloading them onto paper?

What I know now—what I didn't know then—is that this book is my attempt to try to figure out how to forgive. Forgive both what happened to my husband and the physiatrist's behavior afterward.

The reality is, through typing and retyping these sentences, an understanding has made molecular passage into my hands. Made its way all the way up to my heart.

Now I can take it in.

The physiatrist's narrow focus was probably a reflection of his own shock and disbelief. *How could this be? It's never happened before!* If I were a doctor whose procedure resulted in complications and I were in danger of being sued by a patient, I'm sure my focus would be on myself, too. How distressing, frightening even, it must have been for that experienced and competent doctor to find himself—through no malevolent intent and for the first time ever—in such a vulnerable position.

Distress can reduce us to our most primitive selves. Overwhelmed, we become a giant cluster of needs. And neediness is never very attractive. The physiatrist's behavior after the epidural? I suspect the acute strain of the situation drove him to reveal his unloveliest self.

The other doctors, nurses, physical therapists, aides, and administrators we encountered during those years were in a perpetual state of overwhelm. Every single day, suffering surrounds them. Maybe one percent are so stressed, they show their least lovely selves. Just as ninety-nine percent of them, ninety-nine percent of the time, show their loveliest selves.

My behavior? You were right, Mike and Laurie. It's not necessarily a good thing to *always* be guarding against things going wrong. To think of ourselves as being between something awful that has happened and something awful getting ready to happen. When I wasn't faking patience in order to get what I wanted, I was showing *im*patience. Being demanding. I fell into the trap of seeing Henry's caregivers as *other.* As though it was us against them. My unlovely self on full display.

·

Isn't it the same in marriage? Henry knows an uglier Judy than anyone else in the world knows. He knows a more attractive Judy, as well. Just as I know both sides of him.

Marriage. And trauma. They both have a way of introducing us to our most extreme selves.

·

We count on our doctors to keep us from pain, from getting hurt or debilitated or old. Just as we count on our own ingenuity. Jogging is good for our health? Swimming? Fish oil? Check, check, and check. We should stay away from carbs? Fats? Wheat? Dairy? BPA? Well, all right, then.

At some point, though, all our efforts—and the efforts of our doctors—will be insufficient. They might even backfire.

·

Again, similar to marriage. We must scrap the illusion that marrying that one perfect person will end our suffering, bring endless bliss, fix everything.

·

More about blame and forgiveness: If Henry's and my anger should not be directed at the doctor who administered the shot, should we be mad at the systemic secrecy that keeps doctors from speaking freely with their patients, from explaining fully, from openly apologizing?

Well, maybe we patients share the blame when we seek to sue doctors when things go wrong. Lawsuits lead to closed-mouthed doctors. Closed-mouthed doctors lead to lawsuits.

It appears we're all complicit.

·

Final lesson for myself: The doctors, nurses, aides, physical therapists—the whole medical world—could not keep Henry safe. Then again, *I* couldn't keep Henry safe. *Henry* couldn't keep Henry safe.

If it's so unclear who gets the blame, maybe I just need to forgive. The medical people. The system in which they operate. Henry. Myself.

We're all just flawed people—doctors, patients, husbands, wives—hoping to escape the traps that fate sets.

74

It's been eleven years since the epidural. We're eating Sunday-morning breakfast at the glass-top table on the terrace. I usually call it the balcony, but I have a friend who wants me to use the word *terrace*. It sounds *nicer*, she says.

Because the June air is so cool, Henry and I are happy to be in full sun. We're also happy with the spicy fragrance of the blooms dotting the potted magnolias in each corner of the terrace. And we're happy being four stories up; it means we look out on a wide-open sky, blue today. Sometimes, at sunset, it's pink. Henry is reading the Sports section. I've got the Living section.

Two years ago, we sold the redbrick house we'd lived in for thirty-three years and moved up the street to this condo. We're so close we could've carried our queen-sized mattress on our backs. But moving to a condo is not something I ever wanted to do. I thought we'd buy a tiny 1920s bungalow, and I'd live out my days tending hollyhocks and dahlias beside the front door. Henry kept saying why in the world would we trade gutters on one house for gutters on another? Why would we give up one backyard that gets too wet when it rains, only to take on another?

He was right. Just about every day, one of us says to the other, "Don't you just love it here?" Our own private incantation. Just as, this morning, one of us says to the other, "Don't you just love our Sunday breakfast?" We never get tired of eggs scrambled with good cheddar cheese, bacon fried crisp, toast with orange marmalade for me, strawberry preserves for him.

In fact, we often say to each other how fortunate we are to be living this narrative.

There *have* been trips to the ER. Once, he called to me in the middle of the night from the bathroom. He'd gotten up to use the toilet and suddenly couldn't move. He sometimes has intense nerve pain in his good leg. His good, unoperated-on shoulder is not so good. But several times a week, he walks for about twenty minutes in the hall of our building. I hear the galump of his cane each time he passes our door. He still drives, working the brake and gas with his left foot. He does the grocery shopping and most of the errands. You'll find him front-row center at Tess and Benjamin's Saturday afternoon soccer and basketball games. He and I flew to New York recently to see Lucy and Zoe sing at Carnegie Hall with the Young Voices of the Carolinas. Each time he and I navigated a wide avenue, I stationed us on the outer rim of the sidewalk, so that the instant the light changed, we could immediately head across. Too many times we found ourselves in the middle of the street, hobbling along—Henry leaning on his cane, holding my arm—when the light changed and traffic started up. I flashed forward in my mind to the two of us thrown in the gutter, swivel-eyed, the taxi that struck us long gone.

Our lives have definitely changed since that long-ago trip to New York when we glided along the snowy city streets. Still, it's a good life.

.

I don't lay claim to special knowledge, but here's what I'm catching on to:

Nobody is immune to change. We all end up surprising ourselves and our mates.

It may not be a sudden and dramatic change, a kitchen-sink kind of change. (Everything but . . .) Sometimes it's a slow, ordinary change: I now wear glasses. Henry has a beard. A beard with a lot of white in it. I worry even more than I did when I was younger. He snores more. I sleep less. He sleeps more. His jokes, once pristine, now go on too long; I keep telling him to cut the nonessential parts.

On our wedding day, we thought we could see around the next hill. We believed everything would stay the same as the minute the two of us stepped under that orchid- and ivy-covered chuppah. Defying all reason, we looked each other right in the eye and said, Okay, I do. But our vows were a warning we should've taken note of: *Beware! Changes coming!*

But did Henry and I really change?

True, he no longer possesses physical strength. However. Isn't it physical strength that enables him to push against the obstacles blocking his way?

I never saw myself as strong. As far as I could tell, neither did anybody else. I colluded with the people who shared that opinion of me. I'm just now fully acknowledging the strength that was mine all along.

In my twenties, just as I was beginning to trust my own specialness, my pluck, I got married and saw myself settling happily into the role of Yielding Wife. The real truth: As I write this memoir and look back at scenes from our marriage, I don't see a whole lot of yielding going on.

Issues of identity are so key in marriage. *Who am I when I'm with you?* I used to think that if I'd married my high school boyfriend, I'd have been one way. And if I'd married the guy I was engaged to, I'd have been another way. But because I married Henry, I'm this way.

Well, the reality is I was actually Judy all along. Steely, self-assured Judy. Gutsy, even. Because I was raised by the parents you'd pick if you could design your own parents. Parents who thought everything I did was just fine. Now, *that* generates self-confidence in a child. At the same time, this paradox: Even as my parents were believing deeply in my abilities, they were also nurturing my childhood image. (*After all, she's the baby of the family—and so small!*) I grew up with self-confidence, but I also held on to an identity that had been assigned to me—Little Miss Meek,

Little Miss Reliant—a mythologized self that never really existed.

Or maybe it did exist. Or, rather, coexist. Maybe we are always all things—the weak one, the strong one, the angry one, the forgiving one.

·

So many shifts. Shifts in how we see ourselves. Shifts in how we see our mates. Shifts in how each of us operates in the world. And within the marriage.

These shifts do not necessarily cause a marriage to falter. They can strengthen it. If we take the aerial view. And keep creating our marriage as if from scratch. And keep falling into bed with each other.

·

Young love turning into old love.

·

"I'm the lucky one," I say, twisting to turn off the lamp on my bedside table.

"No, I am," Henry says, dropping his book on the floor and flicking off his light.

It's our longest-running ritual, pretending to argue over who's luckier to have gotten the other. Usually, after the Who's Luckier Game, I tell him I had no idea I would get somebody so good-looking. Then he says the same thing to me. But I always answer that he's wrong, I'm not good-looking. Then he insists, yes, you are. I say maybe I was good-looking the year we met, when I was living in New York and wearing eye shadow and mascara.

We meet, face-to-face, in the middle of the bed. I pull at the waist of my pajamas, straightening the twisted pastel cotton. He adjusts his white T-shirt, his blue-and-white striped boxers. Now, that's better. In the violet light from the windows on either side of the bed, I can make out his strong chin. I brush my thumb around his eye. As if stitching, I zigzag my thumb down his cheekbone. We *are* growing old together, after all. I fold my hands into my neck and curl into him. He pulls the down comforter over both of us, then reaches beneath to wrap one arm around me, his palm fitting the curve in the small of my back. His other arm folds under his head. Just like that, I can tell, he's asleep. I feel his breath on my face. I'm not sleeping. Which is fine. Happiness is keeping me awake.

Acknowledgments

So many people are the scaffolding for this book. I feel deep gratitude and love for each of you:

My daughter and son-in-law, Laurie (she helped me with this book in a million different ways) and Bob Smithwick. My son and daughter-in-law, Mike and Brooke Goldman. My grandchildren, Lucy and Zoe Smithwick and Tess and Benjamin Goldman. My brother, Donald Kurtz. And those who are no longer with us: my parents, Margaret (Peggy) and Ben Kurtz; my sister, Brenda Meltsner; Mattie Culp.

My nephews and nieces and cousins and sisters-in-law; my friends (including the Breakfast Group, of course); fellow writers; my book club; yoga pals; neighbors; Table Rock Writers Workshop (colleagues and students). Too many lovely and loving souls to name. But you know who you are. And, surely, you know how much I love and appreciate you.

My eagle-eyed readers: Abigail DeWitt (winner of the award for having read this book the most times), Darnell Arnoult, Dana Sachs, Paul Austin, Betsy Thorpe, Charla Muller, Kim Wright Wiley, Dannye Powell, Peggy Payne. For legal advice: Alice Richey and Jon Buchan.

My editor, Nan Talese: I'm thrilled and honored to be with you. To have heard of you all these years, your stature in the industry, the legend that you are, and then to be given the privilege of working with you, to experience your warmth, gracious nature, your *humanness*—I will never stop feeling thrilled and honored.

The magnificent people at Nan A. Talese/Doubleday and Penguin Random House, especially Carolyn Williams for beautifully and competently ushering my book through; Bette Alexander, editorial production manager, whose eye is so keen; Amy Brosey, copy editor; Michael J. Windsor, jacket designer; Maria Carella, book designer; Charlotte O'Donnell, publicist; Hannah Engler, marketing.

My agent, Grainne Fox: I love the Irish in your voice. I love your enthusiasm. I love your editing skills and kindness and humor. I love that you're my agent. Thank you Veronica Goldstein for your efficiency, your guidance. Thank you both for the title of this book.

In this memoir, I kept to the truth as tightly as I could, relying on the notes I'd taken over the years, medical records, and my memory. But life does not happen in a straight line, so my job—the job of every memoirist—was to marshal random occurrences into a story. If I could not recall a particular detail (a piece of dialogue, for example), I tried to at least capture the spirit. Also, I changed the names and descriptions of some people in order to disguise their identity and protect their privacy. I refashioned letters from a lawyer and a doctor for the same reasons. Above all, I tried my best to be honest and fair.

A Note About the Author

Judy Goldman is the author of two novels, *Early Leaving* and *The Slow Way Back*, which was a finalist for Southern Independent Booksellers Alliance's Novel of the Year and winner of the Sir Walter Raleigh Fiction Award and the Mary Ruffin Poole Award for First Fiction. Her memoir, *Losing My Sister,* was a finalist for both SIBA's Memoir of the Year and *ForeWord Review*'s Memoir of the Year. She is the author of two books of poetry, *Holding Back Winter* and *Wanting to Know the End.* Her work has appeared in *Real Simple, The Washington Post,* and in numerous literary journals and anthologies. Goldman received the Hobson Award for Distinguished Achievement in Arts and Letters and the Fortner Writer and Community Award for Outstanding Generosity to Other Writers and the Larger Community. Born and raised in Rock Hill, South Carolina, she lives in Charlotte, North Carolina. She and her husband have two children and four grandchildren.

A Note on the Type

This book was set in a typeface called Walbaum. The original cutting of this face was made by Justus Erich Walbaum (1768–1839) in Weimar in 1810. The type was revived by the Monotype Corporation in 1934. Young Walbaum began his artistic career as an apprentice to a maker of cookie molds. How he managed to leave this field and become a successful punch cutter remains a mystery. Although the type that bears his name may be classified as modern, numerous slight irregularities in its cut give this face its humane manner.